wild COCKTAILS

wild COCKTAILS

FROM THE MIDNIGHT APOTHECARY

OVER 100 RECIPES USING HOME-GROWN AND FORAGED FRUITS, HERBS, AND EDIBLE FLOWERS

LOTTIE MUIR

CICO BOOKS

LONDON NEW YORK

FOR MY MOTHER, ANN MUIR, WHO I HOPE WOULD HAVE
LOVED MIDNIGHT APOTHECARY.

This edition published in 2019 by CICO Books
An imprint of Ryland Peters & Small Ltd
20–21 Jockey's Fields   341 E 116th St
London WC1R 4BW   New York, NY 10029
www.rylandpeters.com

10 9 8 7 6 5 4 3 2 1

First published in 2015.

A CIP catalog record for this book is available from the Library
of Congress and the British Library.

ISBN: 978-1-78249-794-3

Printed in China

Editor: Helen Ridge
Designer: Geoff Borin
Photography: Kim Lightbody, plus see page 208 for additional credits
Artwork on page 30: Stephen Dew

Editor: Carmel Edmonds
In-house designer: Fahema Khanam
Art director: Sally Powell
Production manager: Gordana Simakovic
Publishing manager: Penny Craig
Publisher: Cindy Richards

**Foraging wild ingredients requires expert knowledge and
identification. The photographs and text in this book should not
be used alone for identification purposes. The author and publisher
cannot be held responsible for, nor shall they be liable for, the
erroneous consumption of wild plants that have caused severe or
allergic reactions resulting from misidentification, nor the
overconsumption of wild plants that have been shown to be toxic
when consumed in large doses.**

CONTENTS

INTRODUCTION

"Wild" conjures images of something uncultivated, uninhibited, and without boundaries. It appeals to me as I hope it does to you. So does the sense of extravagance and enthusiasm. In proportion, wildness creates a feeling of happiness and wellbeing. Overdose on it, though, and it can leave you and those around you feeling nauseous and out of sorts. The analogy applies perfectly to cocktails, wild or otherwise.

The concept of wild cocktails is about extending your cocktail cabinet outdoors, using garden and foraged botanical ingredients to infuse and garnish your cocktails. Whether you have a windowsill, a small outdoor patch, a huge garden, or a desire to forage for free, local wild ingredients, this book will hopefully inspire you to make your own delectable cocktail creations. And if you just want to make some great cocktails using ingredients from your local farmers' market or store, this book is packed with recipes.

For a long time, the cocktail scene was the opposite of wild. OK, it was "wild" in the sense of extravagant and debauched, but for decades, there was very little of note in terms of new ingredients or presentation. The explosion of creativity over the last decade has created a new Golden Age, which is making the cocktail hour rather longer and more exciting. The return to home-grown, local, and organic ingredients is part of its success. Pioneers from the world of gastronomy, mixology, and, in particular, the slow food movement, have learnt techniques and processes from each other. New rituals and traditions are emerging to create incredible cocktails. And the irony is that it is the use of fresh ingredients and techniques from many generations ago that are reinvigorating the cocktail hour—alongside some pretty clever new techniques and processes.

If you factor in the desire to be thrifty as well as decadent, the theme of balance returns. Beauty and thrift, art and science, wholesomeness and revelry—all of them are being used to complement each other. The same is

true with the cocktails themselves. Get the strong, weak, bitter, sweet, and sour elements right, and you're pretty much where you need to be.

Those readers needing to justify the indulgence and expense of a cocktail can turn to history for comfort. Alcohol has been used for over 1,000 years as the most efficient medium for delivering the healing properties of plants into our bloodstream. Records show that distillation has been practiced for medical purposes since the 12th century. By the mid-16th century, apothecaries were the community pharmacists of their day, renowned for their ability to prescribe restorative and healing remedies to their patients. More of us—and many in the pharmaceutical industry—are returning to plants for the answer to our health needs. So you will find in this book some very old recipes for which I can take no credit. They served our ancestors well and have been handed down through the generations.

I've come to cocktails via gardening and foraging. I am the daughter of an avid gardener who turned our inner London Cricklewood vicarage garden in the 1970s into a beautifully designed, almost self-sufficient plot, complete

with an orchard and chickens. I was lucky enough to be given my own little patch of ground in it and was encouraged to forage for wild food under her guidance. From that magical beginning, I had a deep appreciation of "urban farming," the wonder of wild food foraging, and the importance of good design. It was only a matter of time before I turned my attention to drink!

My understanding of cocktails comes from a certain knowledge of plants and a desire to show them off to greatest effect. I have a love of experimenting with alcohol and a desire to enjoy drinking it in as natural a setting as possible.

But the idea of wild cocktails is only partly about using foraged ingredients to infuse and garnish your drinks. Hopefully, it also conveys the sense of wildness about the setting in which we, at Midnight Apothecary, serve our cocktails. Instead of a formal cocktail lounge, we sit around a firepit surrounded by a selection of wild and cultivated plants that are used to infuse and garnish the cocktails. It

is as informal and "natural" as we can make it. The urge to get close to nature is a common cry in any city. The more complicated and sophisticated life becomes, the more we crave simplicity and authenticity. It's a primitive impulse to put our hands in the soil or sit in a circle around a fire. It's simple, ancient, and just feels right. That is all we are doing. And it's the essence of something that is happening all over cities.

I am happier and in a more natural state in my jeans by a firepit, preferring to leave the classy dressing to the garnishes in my cocktail. It turns out I am not alone in this. Many of our guests at Midnight Apothecary love the cozy informality of huddling around the firepit and toasting marshmallows as they sip their cocktails and chat to strangers. The smell of wood smoke on their clothes only seems to add to the experience.

I love micro-worlds, whether it's a rock pool, a mossy tree stump, or something in a glass. If they look and smell right, you can lose yourself in them. Their smell alone can

conjure up strong emotional responses based on memory; for example, a summer's day or a walk in a wood. At their best, cocktails—and gardens—are magical creations that balance wildness and design in an orgy of the senses.

Mae West said too much of a good thing can be wonderful. But, let's face it, it can also render a cocktail undrinkable or unsafe. Indeed, if you are using wild ingredients, it is essential to your wellbeing to know exactly what you are about to imbibe. And in terms of a well-balanced cocktail, it is also essential to understand a few basics about balance and ratios. So, while I hope this book will help your imagination to go wild, it is also intended to provide a few basic principles from the world of mixology, alongside some top tips and safety guidelines on foraging and growing your own cocktail cabinet.

Our recipe at Midnight Apothecary is really very simple. Take one patch of ground. Scatter liberally with seeds and love. Harvest the bounty, stick it in a glass, light a fire, and invite the people. They will come and they will love it!

CHAPTER 1

THE COCKTAIL CABINET

Rather than viewing a cocktail cabinet as a dusty wooden cupboard full of brightly colored, sticky-topped liqueurs that haven't been touched since they were won in a raffle, this book looks at growing one, literally—extending it outdoors so that the plant life around you transforms your cocktail adventures throughout the year. That's not to say that the booze doesn't matter—far from it. You will still need some good-quality base spirits. This is all about bringing some fresh and delicious ingredients into the mix to complement and contrast with the delicious, lovingly crafted booze already available.

In Chapter Two (Cocktail Elements), you will see how to make a huge variety of infusions, syrups, liqueurs, bitters, and garnishes using these fresh ingredients. But to make them, and to garnish the finished cocktail, you will first need to stock up on some essentials—and perhaps a few indulgences. These supplies live more naturally in a pantry or a kitchen than in a bar. If you enjoy cooking, chances are you will already have some of them to hand. The ingredients and flavor combinations are almost exactly the same in the culinary and mixology world.

We're not doing anything new here. The word "apothecary" is derived from the Latin apotheca, which meant a place where wine, spices, and herbs were stored—which is just what you're creating!

THE PANTRY

The ingredients you store in your pantry and refrigerator are the support show to the main act: the booze. The better quality they are, the better the cocktail.

SUGARS You will see throughout the book that all syrups, liqueurs, jams, purées, candied fruit, and some cocktail rims require sugar or a sugar alternative. Superfine (caster) sugar is best for making most syrups, but I use granulated sugar for jams and jellies and, occasionally, for simple syrups if I'm out of superfine. Raw, brown sugar is good for mojitos.

SUGAR ALTERNATIVES Raw local honey has health benefits (see page 188) and also makes an excellent honey syrup in a variety of cocktails, but you may want particular floral honeys for certain flavor profiles. Have a couple of different varieties available. Maple syrup and agave nectar are both great sugar alternatives, provided you understand their properties and limitations (see page 69). Stevia in liquid/processed form may also interest you as a healthy alternative sweetener (see page 69).

SALTS A pinch of salt can counteract bitterness, and small grains of table salt are perfect for that. Salt rims can be a good way to enhance the flavor of a drink with a savory component, as well as looking and feeling attractive. Try to find good-quality kosher or sea salt for rims or be more extravagant with pink Himalayan mountain salt, black salt (see right), and smoked salt. These can all be found at specialty food stores or online catering suppliers.

EDIBLE GRADE ESSENTIAL OILS These are very expensive but add an intense, pure flavor of the ingredient in question to a spirit, such as jasmine in the Chelsea Fringe Collins (see page 116). A lot of specialized equipment and over 8,000 blossoms are required to make 5mg of the essential oil, which makes it a viable alternative to preparing the raw ingredient yourself.

MILK AND CREAM Sometimes you will want a mild, smooth element in a cocktail and a luxurious, creamy, and frothy texture. Egg white does the trick in Sours and a few other cocktails, but very thick milk or, better still, heavy (double) cream with a high-fat content is what's required in some fizzes, where that extra dimension of texture and viscous mouth-feel is required.

TEA Disposable tea bags are a great way of infusing flavor into liquor and spirits without the fuss of straining. They can even be used as an ingredient to smoke spirits. Loose tea can obviously also be used for smoking (see Bacon and Tea, Smoke-infused Whisky, page 39) or infusing cocktails but will, of course, require straining in infusions.

Black salt

EGGS Your cocktails will not taste of eggs if you use them, I promise. Eggs provide a tasteless and smooth cocktail foam (see page 36), giving your drink a frothy and creamy mouth-feel and a great surface area on which to place a garnish or add a couple of drops of bitters. They also add a mild element if you need to balance the strong, the sweet, and the sour. Use organic eggs, as fresh as you can get them.

VINEGAR You can provide a wonderful umami, savory taste with the right balance of acidic and sweet using aged balsamic vinegar (see Salad Days, page 138). A good apple cider or champagne vinegar wouldn't go amiss in some shrubs, too, like the Raspberry and Scented Geranium Shrub (see page 105).

SPICES There is a danger of storing so many herbs and spices that they go past their shelf life without being used. However, a few well-sealed spices, such as cinnamon, nutmeg, star anise, and whole cloves, can never go amiss, particularly in the fall and winter when you are out of many fresh herbs and want warming infusions and garnishes to pair with punchy dark spirits like whiskey and rum. Ginger is a great fresh spice to have to hand. Other useful fresh spices (and herbs) are listed on pages 21 and 23.

GELATIN This odorless, tasteless thickening agent is used in foams (see page 36). It is sold in dried sheets, or leaves, which dissolve more slowly than the granulated type, but produce a clearer, gelled product. They come in bronze, silver, gold, and platinum strength—I use platinum. Since gelatin is derived from animal hide and bone, it is not acceptable for certain diets. Alternatives include agar, a seaweed-based replacement. You can use agar in the same way but, as it gels at a higher temperature, you may need less to achieve the same texture of foam. Agar is available online and at many Asian grocers.

BITTERS This is an essential component of many cocktails (see pages 96–97). You can make your own (see Wild Cherry Bitters, pages 102–103) or have a couple of classic bitters to hand. Use a good-quality brand. Angostura and orange bitters are the two I use the most in this book, but there has been an explosion in the number of small-batch bitters produced in a huge variety of flavors, if you want to experiment.

The bacteria that causes salmonella is usually on the outside of the shell. If this concerns you, rinse your eggs in a bowl of cold water with a couple of tablespoons of bleach. Rinse them off under a running faucet (tap), dry, and store in the refrigerator until you need them.

If you need to avoid raw eggs, use pasteurized, powdered, or carton egg white instead: 2 teaspoons of powder and 2 tablespoons of water per egg white. If you are vegan, try dissolving 1 tablespoon of plain agar powder in 1 tablespoon of water and follow the instructions on the packet.

HERBS Dried herbs provide a stronger flavor than fresh; when making infusions, you need a third of the amount. Dried herbs are handy if you want to use them out of season or you need a herb that doesn't grow near you, such as wild hibiscus (see page 124). Herb flowers have their most intense oil concentration and flavor just after the flower buds appear but before they open.

SODA WATER AND MIXERS Many cocktails, particularly long drinks served in a Collins glass, require carbonated mixers. This is the weak (but vital) element of the cocktail, alongside ice, to contrast with the strong element of the drink: the booze. I primarily use soda water. Essentially, it is water mixed with sodium bicarbonate (carbon dioxide). The difference with sparkling mineral water is that it contains naturally occurring sodium bicarbonate but also a lot of other minerals that can affect the taste of cocktails—hence soda water or seltzer being the preferred mixer. To be honest, I wouldn't get too worked up about it; my main concern is to use the contents of small bottles in one go, so the water doesn't go flat.

For many gin lovers, tonic water is the "go-to," non-negotiable mixer, with a distinctive bitter flavor due to the quinine. It does, indeed, make a perfect match with gin's strong juniper and herbal notes. As it is such an important element of the drink, it is worth investing in a good-quality brand, such as Fever-Tree.

CITRUS The essential acid component in many cocktails, to balance the sweet, derives from citrus. Organic, unwaxed lemons, limes, grapefruit, and oranges are all wonderful additions to your cocktails. Lemons provide a distinct lemon color, have a very clean, crisp flavor, and are less acidic than limes, with a pH of 2.2–2.5. Their white pith is extremely bitter. Limes, on the other hand, have a pH of 1.8–2, a green-colored juice, almost no pith, and a herbal complexity to the flavor. While some people say that limes are more suited to herbal/vegetal cocktails, I vary the use of lemons and limes depending on the amount of acidity I want and the color of the final drink. Experiment by making the same cocktail first with lemon and then with lime. See which you prefer. There is no right or wrong answer, but to balance the drink you may need to add a drop, more or less, of a sweetener, depending on whether you are using lemon or lime. If you are lucky enough to find bergamots, yuzu, or other exotic citrus, use them as inspiration for some divine seasonal cocktails.

To dry freshly picked herbs, spread them out on paper towels or a dishtowel until any moisture has evaporated. Then tie them into small bundles by their stems and hang upside down in a warm, dry, airy place out of the sun, with plenty of air circulation around each bunch. You can also dry herbs on baking sheets in an oven on the lowest possible setting. They are ready when they are brittle and crumble easily. Store dried herbs in a cool, dry place away from sunlight, moisture, and heat. Many herbs can be kept for a year if stored properly.

To dry herb seeds, such as fennel, tie the stems but place the heads in a brown paper bag with a few holes in the sides. Suspend the bag somewhere dark with good air circulation and collect the seeds when they are fully dry. Store the dried seeds in airtight containers away from sunlight.

Fresh herbs can be frozen in ice trays filled with water. Transfer them to airtight containers or plastic bags once they have frozen. They will not be any good as a garnish but are fine for infusions. You can also store many leaves and berries whole by allowing them to freeze on a baking sheet in the freezer and then keeping them frozen in a Ziploc bag.

THE BOOZE

Obviously you will need some booze—we are not in the business of making hooch here. Depending on your level of ambition and budget, you will need some base spirits to infuse or accompany your flowers, leaves, roots, spices, and citrus. Hopefully, these will have been lovingly created with a variety of organic ingredients themselves. With the exception of vodka, they will already be laden with flavor from the grain, vegetable, fruit, or sugar product with which they were made, together with the flavor they take on from specific aging processes. In the case of gin, you will be competing with several, possibly many, botanicals, depending on the type of gin you choose. Spirits are expensive, so start with a few mid-range ones and see how you enjoy their flavor when paired with your seasonal harvests.

VODKA The word "vodka" comes from *voda*, which is translated from both Russian and Polish as water. It is thought to have originated in the 14th century in Eastern Europe as, you guessed it, a medicine. By U.S. government definition, vodka must be a "neutral spirit... without distinctive character, aroma, taste, or color." By definition, then, it doesn't have much flavor. It is traditionally made from grains or potatoes but almost anything that will ferment can be used. Black Cow vodka, distilled in Dorset, southwest England, is made from whey, a byproduct of cow's milk, and is certainly very smooth. Vodka connoisseurs will tell you how much creamier/spicier/sweeter certain vodkas are but, to be honest, I am more interested in the level of alcohol: the proof or ABV (alcohol by volume). You are looking for a vodka that is a minimum of 100 proof (50% ABV) or higher. This provides the perfect neutral-tasting spirit that is strong enough to extract the flavors and other herbal constituents of your chosen leaves/spices/petals/roots/citrus and to preserve them safely.

GIN Gin is altogether more complicated to work with—and delicious. It is essentially vodka that has been infused with juniper (always) and a whole range of botanicals, depending on the particular gin, from citrus to coriander seeds, and roses. Some gins contain over 20 botanicals. Originally, gin was, you guessed it, a medicine, invented around 1650 in the Netherlands by a Dr. Sylvius, as a remedy for kidney and stomach disorders using the oil of juniper (*Juniperus communis*) in a base grain spirit.

There is a flourishing of small-scale distilleries around the world, particularly in London, which have gone back to original recipes or created brand-new ones using cultivated or wild botanicals. We are very lucky at Midnight Apothecary to be just around the corner from Jensen, distillers who make both London Dry Gin and Old Tom, the latter slightly sweeter with more botanicals and based on a very particular 1840's recipe.

SCOTCH There are two types of Scotch whisky (not whiskey). Blended Scotch is a blend of malt and grain whisky. Single malt whisky is made in one distillery from malted barley. The flavor of each malt differs from distillery to distillery, depending on a number of factors, such as climate, water source, local wild yeasts, the shape of the still, to name but a few. Both single malt and blended Scotch must be matured in oak barrels for at least three years. It is sweet and smooth with complex flavors, including additional savory, salty, and bitter notes.

WHISKEY Let's keep things simple. There are a variety of ingredients and distillation methods but we'll just stick to the major taste differences. Unlike vodka, which is produced at a high proof (ABV) and then processed to remove all the flavor, whiskey is distilled at a low proof, in order to retain all its flavor, and then aged in wood to create yet another layer of flavor. Yep, this was also originally a medicine, used as an internal anesthetic and an external antibiotic.

BOURBON It is the corn (a minimum of 51%, legally) that gives bourbon the sweetness you either like or don't. It must be matured in new charred oak barrels but there is no specific time requirement for this. The remaining percentage will be made up of other grains, either malted barley, wheat, or rye. Wheat is known for providing a sweet, inoffensive smoothness.

RYE Rye whiskey is known for being spicier and not so sweet as bourbon.

IRISH WHISKEY Irish whiskey uses primarily the same ingredients and methods as blended Scotch whisky, but is obviously made in Ireland. It is distilled three times, instead of twice for Scotch, resulting in a lighter, more delicate flavor. Peat is almost never used in the malting process, so you very rarely get the smoky, earthy notes common to many Scotches.

CANADIAN WHISKEY Canadian whiskey is a blend of grain whiskey with bourbon, rye, or malt. Nine percent of the blend may be made from whiskies from another country or even from distilled fruit juices, hence its reputation for being lighter in body.

EAU DE VIE/BRANDY/COGNAC The difference between eau de vie, brandy, and cognac is, as for many spirits, largely down to oak and time. Eau de vie is a fresh distilled spirit, fermented and double-distilled, then usually bottled immediately (though not always) to preserve the aroma and freshness of the original fruit. Brandy is a distilled spirit (essentially an eau de vie) that is usually made from grapes or grape wine and then aged in wooden barrels (usually oak) to alter its taste and color. Cognac is a well-known brandy made in a very particular way, in a very particular region of France (Cognac!), using a particular type of oak. It is also aged for a minimum of two years to enhance the color and taste. You don't need to use cognac to be assured of a quality brandy, but you can be assured of a unique and uniform taste. Pisco, a grape brandy made in Peru and Chile, is becoming very popular. There are also

many apple brandies, such as calvados, applejack, and Somerset brandy.

RUM Rum is made from the fermented juice of sugarcane molasses and/or other sugarcane byproducts. It can be aged in oak barrels and, therefore, be heavy-bodied and dark, or unaged and, therefore, light or white. The white and gold rums are quite light-bodied with only a slight molasses taste, whereas gold rum has more pronounced sweet molasses notes. Dark rum is much sweeter, with additional flavor and color coming from the aging process, as you would expect. Spiced rum is infused with spices such as cinnamon, vanilla bean (pod), clove, ginger, wormwood, fennel, coffee, and licorice.

TEQUILA Tequila is made from the heart of the Mexican blue agave (*Agave tequilana*). Try to find a tequila made from 100% Mexican blue agave—it won't have a load of caramel and sugar added to mask its inferiority. It will taste a lot better and make those awful, tequila-related hangovers a thing of the past, if drunk in moderation, of

THE MIXERS

It is worthwhile having a few quality mixers (see below) to hand, come the moment you decide to get making cocktails! But I would advise holding off buying them until the moment you actually need them, because they can easily go stale as they lurk at the back of your cocktail cabinet. In fact, once you've opened vermouth—a fortified wine—put it in the refrigerator and consume within a couple of months.

Vermouth: Dry, sweet, red (see pages 98–99)

Bitters: Bitter and aromatic herbs, tinctured in high-proof spirits

Orgeat: An almond mixer—or you can use Sloe Blossom Syrup (see page 93)

Flower water: Orange and rose—a few drops will enhance a variety of cocktails with floral notes

course! I tend to use Reposado or Añejo tequila, which means it has rested and aged in a wooden barrel. If you want a clear cocktail, use Blanco/Silver tequila, which has been aged for only a very short time.

MEZCAL The smoky scents and flavors of mezcal come from the wood used to heat the stones that, in turn, heat the hearts of agave in underground pits. Mezcal connoisseurs can detect notes of chili pepper, chocolate, ash, wood, and fire. Variations occur in the smoke notes according to the type and amount of wood used, as well as the size of the ovens.

CACHAÇA The prized national drink of Brazil is produced by fermenting sugarcane, rather than molasses, which is the case with most other rums. It is a fresh-tasting spirit that, like most types of liquor, varies hugely in quality. Leblon cachaça is one of the good ones, with notes of fruit, herbs, pepper, oak, and vanilla.

GROWING YOUR COCKTAIL CABINET

Whether it's some wild cherries picked in your local park, a section of horseradish root you've dug from the vegetable patch, or some seasonal fruit bought at the local market, these natural treasures provide the inspiration and seasonal element of your cocktail cabinet. These unprocessed ingredients can look, smell, feel, and taste wonderful—as all cocktails should. Usually, the shorter the distance they have had to travel, the fresher, more nutrient-rich, and tastier they will be. They are going to feature in your infused spirits, syrups, liqueurs, bitters, and garnishes.

Painted sage

TO GROW OR NOT TO GROW

You don't need a large yard to grow your cocktail cabinet. A sunny windowsill will allow you to grow a huge variety of Mediterranean and sun-loving herbs for drying or freezing (see page 15) to use all year round. Evergreen plants such as lavender, rosemary, scented geraniums (*Pelargonium*), and sage will provide you with leaves and/or flowers for many months of the year. Slightly shady spots are perfectly suited to mints, basils, lemon verbena, and lemon balm. I would also aim to grow those plants that are difficult for you to buy locally. A few flowers that work beautifully in edible garnishes will also brighten up your surroundings. Nasturtiums, dianthus, jasmine, honeysuckle, cornflowers, marigolds, snapdragons, and love-in-the-mist provide color and/or scent for you, as well as your drinks.

Borage

GARDEN FLOWERS These showstoppers not only look but also taste fantastic.

Borage (*Borago officinalis*)
Bee balm (*Monarda didyma*)
Daylily (*Hemerocallis* species)
Dianthus (*Dianthus* species)
Electric daisy (*Acmella oleracea*)
Fennel (*Foeniculum vulgare*)
Honeysuckle (*Lonicera periclymenum*)
Hollyhock (*Alcea rosea*)
Jasmine (*Jasminum* species)
Lavender (*Lavandula* species)
Marigold (*Calendula officinalis*)
Nasturtium (*Tropaeolum* species)
Rose (*Rosa* species)
Snapdragon (*Antirrhinum majus*)

Jasmine

GARDEN HERBS Many of these plants provide delicious young leaves and shoots for infusions. Later on in the season, they flower. While the leaves won't be as flavorsome after the plants have flowered, the flowers themselves provide a beautiful edible garnish. If you have space, keep most herbs regularly cut for young leaf growth, but let a few grow to seed for flower garnishes. This will also enable you to collect the seed for next year's sowing.

Agastache, anise hyssop (*Agastache foeniculum*)
Basil (*Ocimum basilicum*)
Bee balm (*Monarda didyma*)
Garlic chives (*Allium tuberosum*)
Mint, spearmint, chocolate mint (*Mentha* species)
Sage, blackcurrant, broad-leaved, painted, pineapple, tricolor (*Salvia* species)
Thyme (*Thymus* species)
Lavender (*Lavandula angustifolia* 'Munstead', *L. × intermedia* 'Provence')
Lemon balm (*Melissa officinalis*)
Lemon verbena (*Aloysia triphylla*)
Nasturtium (*Tropaeolum* species)
Rosemary (*Rosmarinus* species)
Scented geranium (*Pelargonium* species)

FORAGING

There's a simple primitive pleasure in knowing you can find, identify, and gather the ingredients for your own food (and drink) in the middle of the city or in a hedgerow near your home. It not only keeps you alive to the joys and drama of nature on your doorstep, but you also get to know the plant life of an area intimately over a few seasons and pay closer attention to its rhythms and life cycle as it yields gluts of different treasures for short periods every year.

Foraging is a great way to add new flavors and visual flair to your cocktails, not to mention nutrients and healing properties. Our palate is accustomed to quite a narrow range of well-known flavors, but if you taste gorse flowers in Gorse Flower Syrup (see page 76), meadowsweet in Meadowsweet Syrup (see page 86), or beech leaves in Beech Leaf Noyau (see page 100), you'll be experiencing something new and exciting.

The delayed gratification of a seasonal bounty—from young shoots to flowers and, finally, seeds—leads to a greater pleasure on their arrival than if you were able to enjoy them all year round. The early celery-like shoots of Alexanders provide very attractive, edible swizzle sticks for a Rhubarbra Collins (see page 131)—much better than a mouth-contorting raw rhubarb spear—while their buds make an attractive garnish and their seeds, later in summer, are an interesting celery-seed-like addition to your cocktails.

THE DOS AND DON'TS

There is a legal gray area about foraging, especially as its popularity is growing. In several areas, such as the ancient forests in the U.K., mushrooms are being picked on such a scale that the ecosystem is being harmed and the authorities are clamping down on foraging. In general, the law says that if you are foraging for your own use and not for commercial purposes, you are entitled to go ahead. There will be exceptions to that if the habitat or species you are interested in is rare and under threat. Always obey the laws that cover conservation in the area you are intending to forage. And make sure you are allowed, or have gained permission, to be on the land you are on. In the U.S., laws vary from state to state, so foragers need to understand and follow state laws. Likewise, Canadians should familiarize themselves with provincial laws.

Take only as much as you need for your own use. During fruit and berry picking seasons, you will often see fruit trees burgeoning with apples, pears, or quinces, not just in wild or public spaces, but in people's front yards, for example. Ask if you can help yourself—most people are reasonable and delighted to let you, even if it is just for the windfall fruits that are lying on the ground. It doesn't do any harm to offer to pick some extra for them.

Obviously a couple of notes of caution are to be sounded if you start to forage for your own ingredients. It is vital that you identify the plants correctly, so you will need a good, pocket-sized wild plant identification book that you can carry with you. To begin with, take

SAFETY FIRST

Wild plants are powerful—they can heal you, but they can also kill you. Always err on the side of caution if you are not completely sure of your find, or if you are pregnant, breast-feeding, on medication, prone to allergies, or elderly.

Wild plants can carry pollutants if you pick too close to a dog-walking area and where farm pesticides or weed killer may have been used.

Avoid foraging in cemeteries because of the possibility of arsenic poisoning dating back to old embalming practices.

your foraged pickings home and cross-reference your finds with another, more comprehensive book or website (see Resources, pages 202–204) before using an ingredient. Join a guided foraging walk with an expert if you get a chance.

GOING WILD

The joy of foraging over the course of a few seasons is that you will notice the same wild plant will reward you with completely different ingredients at different times of the year. Take the humble blackthorn or sloe (*Prunus spinosa*). From the clouds of snowy white blossom that burst onto the scene to herald the beginning of spring you can make a delicate but heady, almond-tasting syrup (see Sloe Blossom Syrup, page 93). Straight after, in mid-spring, you can gather the leaves to make Epiné (see page 63). Finally, from the beginning of fall until mid-winter, you can use the wonderful, ripe, blue-black sloe berries for Sloe Gin (see page 62). Here are just a few of the wild treasures you can use to infuse and garnish your cocktails:

Alexanders

WILD HERBS

Agastache, anise hyssop (*Agastache foeniculum*): flowers, leaves

Alexanders (*Smyrnium olusatrum*): shoots, stalks, buds

Angelica (*Angelica archangelica*): leaves, stems, shoots, seeds

Borage (*Borago officinalis*): leaves, flowers

Chamomile (*Chamaemelum nobile*): flowers

Chervil (*Anthriscus cerefolium*): leaves

Fennel (*Foeniculum vulgare*): stems, fronds, flowers, seeds

Ground ivy (*Glechoma hederacea*): leaves, flowers

Herb bennet (*Geum urbanum*): root

Hogweed (*Heracleum sphondylium*): seeds

Horseradish (*Armoracia rusticana*): root

Juniper (*Juniperus* species): berries

Meadowsweet (*Filipendula ulmaria*): blossom

Mugwort (*Artemisia vulgaris*): leaves

Milk thistle (*Silybum marianum*): root, seeds

Red clover (*Trifolium pratense*): blossom

Sweet cicely (*Myrrhis odorata*): leaves

Sweet woodruff (*Galium odoratum*): leaves, flowers

Tansy (*Tanacetum vulgare*): leaves

Wild thyme (*Thymus serpyllum*): leaves, flowers

Wood sorrel (*Oxalis acetosella*): leaves, flowers

Water mint (*Mentha aquatica*): leaves

White dead nettle (*Lamium album*): flowers

Yarrow (*Achillea millefolium*): leaves, flowers

WILD SHRUBS
Here, I mean "shrub" in the botanical sense—as in bushes—not the vinegar syrup (see page 104)!

Barberry (*Berberis vulgaris, B. canadensis, B. darwinii*): flowers, berries

Blackthorn (*Prunus spinosa*): blossom, leaves, berries

Blackberry (*Rubus fruticosus*): berries

Dog rose (*Rosa canina*): petals, hips

Elder (*Sambucus nigra*): flowers, berries

Gorse (*Ulex europaeus*): flowers

Hawthorn (*Crataegus monogyna*): blossom, berries

Honeysuckle (*Lonicera periclymenum*): blossom, NOT berries

Japanese rose (*Rosa rugosa*): petals, hips

Lilac (*Syringa vulgaris*): flowers

Mahonia (specifically, the Oregon grape, *M. aquifolium*): berries

Raspberry (*Rubus idaeus*): berries

Sumac (all varieties of the genus *Rhus* but NOT poison sumac, *Toxicodendron vernix*, which must be avoided, for obvious reasons): berries

TREE TREASURES

Apples (*Malus* species): blossom, fruit
Beech (*Fagus sylvatica*): leaves
Birch (*Betula alba, B. pendula*): sap
Cherry (*Prunus cerasus, P. serrulata, P.* 'Shogetsu'): blossom, fruit
Cherry plum (*Prunus cerasifera*): fruit
Crab apple (*Malus sylvestris*): fruit
Damson (*Prunus domestica* ssp. *insititia*)
Douglas fir (*Pseudotsuga menziesii*): needles
False acacia/black locust (*Robinia pseudoacacia*): blossom
Lime/linden (*Tilia* x *europaea, T. americana*): blossom, nuts
Medlar (*Mespilus germanica*): fruit
Magnolia (*Magnolia* species): petals
Pear (*Pyrus* species): fruit
Plum (*Prunus* species): fruit
Quince (*Cydonia oblonga*): fruit
Rowan/mountain ash (*Sorbus aucuparia*): berries
Walnut (*Juglans regia*): nuts

False acacia

WILD FLOWERS
We use these edible beauties primarily for garnishes, although many of them can form the base of a syrup or spirit infusion.

Chervil (*Anthriscus cerefolium*)
Chicory (*Cichorium intybus*)
Coltsfoot (*Tussilago farfara*)
Common mallow (*Malva sylvestris*)
Dandelion (*Taraxacum officinale*)
Dog rose (*Rosa canina*)
Fennel (*Foeniculum vulgare*)
Goldenrod (*Solidago virgaurea*)
Ground ivy (*Glechoma hederacea*)
Heartsease (*Viola tricolor*)
Honeysuckle (*Lonicera periclymenum*)
Oxeye daisy (*Leucanthemum vulgare*)
Primrose (*Primula vulgaris*)
Red clover (*Trifolium pratense*)
Sweet violet (*Viola odorata*)
Vetch (*Vicia* species)
Viper's bugloss (*Echium vulgare*)
Wild mustard (*Sinapis arvensis*)
Yarrow (*Achillea millefolium*)

Dog rose

FORAGING EQUIPMENT

Sturdy scissors/garden clippers/penknife. (The acceptable length of a penknife varies from state to state in the U.S. and from country to country—in the U.K., for example, it is 3in/76mm and the knife should not be capable of being locked in the open position. Make sure you stay within the law of your state/province/country. Err on the side of caution and certainly do not enter any public buildings with anything that can be construed as a blade.)

★

Sturdy gardening gloves

★

Canvas bag

★

Walking stick/pole with curved end to pull on branches laden with hard-to-reach fruit or nuts

★

Hat to shade your eyes from thorns and strong sun

★

Small, individual, breathable baskets (such as wicker), boxes, or bags for different berries/leaves/flowers—you don't want to waste time laboriously separating them out when you get home

★

Labels and/or a waterproof pen to make a note of what, where, and when for particular finds

★

Band-Aids for the inevitable thorny cuts!

★

Damp cloth or tissue in an opaque sealable box for storing flowers and leaves without them wilting

★

Brush to remove soil/debris/wildlife before putting your treasures in a basket, so you don't have to wash them later

FORAGING TECHNIQUES

There are some absolute rules you should follow in the interests of foraging responsibly and sustainably:

Always leave plenty of a plant behind to allow it to regenerate.

★

Never pick anything by the root if you are foraging on someone else's land and have not been given express permission to do so.

★

Never pick anything you know to be endangered or rare.

★

Pick only enough for yourself, not the whole neighborhood.

★

Pick a few leaves, berries, or blossoms from one plant and move on to another, so that one plant isn't stripped.

★

Take care not to trample over tender plants.

★

Always leave plenty behind for other users of that plant: bees, butterflies, birds, insects and, mammals.

★

Use a pair of garden clippers, sharp scissors, or a penknife, so you don't damage the plant by tearing it.

★

Again, and most importantly, with regards to identification, IF IN DOUBT, LEAVE IT OUT.

BASIC KITCHEN EQUIPMENT

If you are going to get busy with syrups, liqueurs, and other infusions, you will need some basic equipment, much of which you are likely to have anyway if you are a foodie. They are all available from quality gourmet stores and online catering suppliers.

BLENDER Use one that has the option of varying speeds and a reasonable-sized jar, so that you don't have to do many different batches.

BOTTLES AND JARS Choose a selection of wide-mouthed, sealable glass jars, such as Mason or Kilner jars. A range of sizes, from small glass jar sizes through to 1 pint (500ml), 1 quart (1 liter), 1½ quarts (1½ liters), and ½ gallon (2 liters), will be useful.

COFFEE FILTERS These do the same job as muslin or cheesecloth for straining very fine particles from an infusion, leaving you with a clear, sediment-free liquid.

COFFEE GRINDER For grinding spices.

FINE-MESH STRAINER Like a chinois, for straining very small particles from infusions.

FUNNEL Use one which is thin enough to fit inside a presentation bottle.

GLASS PRESENTATION BOTTLES Ranging from ½ pint (250ml), 1 pint (500ml) to 1 quart (1 liter).

HAND-HELD SMOKER Smoking your infusions, cocktails, or even ice cubes can add a richness, complexity, and depth of flavor (see Resources, pages 202–204).

HEAVY-BOTTOMED, NONREACTIVE SAUCEPANS When using acidic ingredients, such as citrus juice, fruit, strongly colored vegetables, and brown sugar, use stainless steel, enamel, or lined copper; do not use aluminum, tin, or unlined copper because the lining of your pan will become stained and possibly pit and peel off.

JELLY BAG This purpose-made, fine-mesh bag is used for straining the juice from cooked fruit.

MUSLIN/CHEESECLOTH For getting a liquid as clear and particle-free as possible. Fold 3-ft (1-m) squares of muslin or cheesecloth into at least two or three layers thick and place inside a fine-mesh strainer, like a chinois. Ensure they are clean prior to use—they are washable and can be used repeatedly.

STERILIZING FLUID This is optional but makes sterilizing a large number of jars in a tub or sink that much easier.

WIDE-MOUTHED PITCHER Used for funneling infusions from a pan.

Muslin, chinois, and Kilner jar

MAKING THE COCKTAILS

While it is perfectly possible to improvise with ordinary glasses, pitchers, and spoons, there are a few pieces of inexpensive equipment that make the whole business of cocktails more of a spectacle, easy, and fun. Most of these items can be bought in gourmet cooking stores or online, but there are plenty of secondhand and vintage suppliers if you want a more classic look.

BARSPOON While you can use a long wooden spoon or a teaspoon for the various functions of a barspoon, it's worth getting this one item of equipment for all the tasks it can do in one. It is great for stirring, mixing, scooping, and muddling. Use a stainless-steel one with a long, twisted, thin handle, which allows the spoon to spin freely in your hand while you are stirring drinks, and a disc welded to the end. This allows you to muddle fruit and "layer" drinks by slowly pouring the liquid over the disc. Try to get a barspoon that holds 1 teaspoon (5ml), because you can use it as an additional measure.

BAR TOWELS Lint-free cotton is perfect for keeping glassware sparkling (as is a drop of vinegar in your washing-up water), but a number of bar towels for cleaning down work areas are vital.

CITRUS PRESS A simple hand-held citrus press will make light work of lemon, lime, and small orange juicing. Simply halve the fruit and squeeze but, for accuracy's sake, pour the juice into a measure first, not directly into the glass. Always roll and massage the citrus along a work surface first to extract more juice before you squeeze.

COCKTAIL SHAKER There are two main types of shaker. The common Cobbler shaker is made up of three parts: a pierced lid that acts as an integrated strainer, a tall glass or metal beaker, and a cap that covers the strainer. The Boston shaker is the professional's choice, consisting simply of a pint-sized mixing glass and a slightly larger metal tin that fits over it. It also requires a separate strainer. With either shaker, simply add your cocktail ingredients, fill two-thirds of the way up with ice, and cover with the cap or metal tin. The Boston shaker tin is a good indicator of when a drink is cold enough because it becomes frosty.

CUTTING BOARD AND SHARP KNIFE These are essential for preparing your ingredients behind the bar.

FINE GRATER A small Microplane grater will grate citrus zest and spices like nutmeg and chocolate with supreme ease and finesse, and will prevent bitter pith getting in your drink. It is a great time-saving and useful piece of kit when using citrus in volume, as in something like Limoncello (see page 58).

HAWTHORNE STRAINER A hawthorne strainer is designed to fit perfectly over the mouth of a Boston shaker once you have shaken your cocktail. It is a stainless-steel strainer with a spring-loaded coil around the perimeter to hold back the ice and large pieces of fruit and herbs as you pour your cocktail into the prepared glass.

ICE BUCKET A non-essential item, but, if you are going to be making cocktails for a large group of people, you may want to consider getting one. The vintage world beckons.

ICE SCOOP While your nearest and dearest may not mind your mucky paws being used to fill their glass with ice, others may prefer a more hygienic method. An ice scoop also prevents frostbitten fingers. Try to find a scoop that can nearly fill a pint glass in a single scoop.

JIGGER It is vital to be accurate when pouring cocktails—balance is key and can be easily knocked out by sloppy pouring. A jigger (see right) is made up of two "thimbles" joined together and is used for precise measuring. One thimble is a 1-oz (30-ml) "pony shot," while the other holds a 1½-oz (45-ml) "standard shot" or "jigger." You can also find glass jiggers with calibrated measurements for small additions of liquid. Mixing spoons with ½-oz (15-ml) measures are also useful.

JULEP STRAINER This is the classic strainer for Juleps and is intended to remain in the glass while you drink, to hold back the crushed ice. It is an attractive, domed metal spoon studded with holes and fits inside a Boston shaker or regular mixing glass. It is also used to strain other drinks that are stirred, as opposed to shaken, in a mixing glass.

MIXING GLASS If you have a Boston shaker, you will already own a mixing glass. But, if you want to get fancy with your vintage look, there are plenty of attractive ones out there.

MUDDLER A wooden muddler is the classic version of this cocktail implement. Make sure it is tall and skinny enough to fit in your tallest and skinniest glasses. You can use the disc end of a barspoon or the end of a wooden spoon instead.

PIPETTE You can buy very cheap plastic pipettes from a pharmacy. They enable you to add drops or splashes of a syrup to the bottom of a glass, once you have built up the drink, to create a layered color effect (see Chelsea Fringe Collins, page 116).

PROFESSIONAL CREAM WHIPPER (with N2O cartridges) Not absolutely necessary but a lot of fun and perfect for instant infusions and unctuous, creamy cocktail foams (see page 36).

PUNCH BOWL Punch is becoming very trendy again. There is no reason why you can't serve it in a large pitcher or bowl but there are many beautiful vintage ones out there that would make a great centerpiece on the bar.

Jigger

TEA STRAINER Sometimes you will need an additional strainer to double-strain your cocktail and catch really tiny particles of ice, herbs, or fruit that won't be caught by the shaker's strainer or hawthorne/julep strainer. A regular, small tea strainer does this job very well.

TWEEZERS/TONGS Not essential but useful for handling intricate edible flowers or herbs in a long, thin glass. You will need extra-long and skinny ones, the kind used by sushi/sous chefs, in order to reach the bottom of your glass.

VEGETABLE PEELER An invaluable and cheap piece of equipment likely to be owned by you already. Perfect for preparing a lemon twist garnish.

GLASSWARE

Finding the perfect glasses is easily addictive, especially if you have access to thrift stores and vintage markets. Using the right glass for a particular drink doesn't just look good—the size and shape of the glass also serve a specific purpose.

Choose a glass based on how big the drink will be and whether it will have ice cubes in it. For example, if you are making a garden cocktail with soda water over ice, filled with edible flowers and herbs, a tall, narrow Collins glass is ideal because you can mount ice cubes one on top of the other up the glass, pushing the flowers and herbs to the sides, rather than losing them from view in a wider glass. It also takes longer for the ice to melt if you fill up the whole glass with ice.

It is important that the glass looks reasonably full, so it is better to serve a Martini straight up without ice in a small 5-oz (150-ml) glass than in a 9-oz (270-ml) glass, which either looks mean if you don't fill it or renders your guest legless if you do. Smaller glasses allow you to serve smaller quantities of high-quality spirits and mixers, which encourages responsible drinking and makes for a much more pleasurable drinking experience.

CHAMPAGNE FLUTE
Long, narrow-stemmed glass used to serve sparkling wine. I serve my Bellinis in these and, of course, the French 75 (see page 172).

COLLINS/HIGHBALL (1)
This is the glass of choice for a long drink with a mixer served over ice. Typically, a Collins glass is slightly taller and narrower than a highball, holding 10–14oz (300–420ml), whereas a highball is usually 8–10oz (240–300ml). I typically use a 12-oz (360-ml) Collins.

COUPE (SAUCER) (2)
Very attractive, bowl-shaped champagne glass that is now popular for serving Martinis, Sours, and other cocktails. We use a 5-oz (150-ml) glass.

JULEP CUP (3)
A metal cup made of pewter, silver, or copper and, as the name suggests, the perfect vessel for a Julep. The metal becomes wonderfully frosted as it chills.

MARTINI (4)
Also known as a cocktail glass, this is the classic, cone-shaped glass with a stem, holding 3–12oz (90–360ml). I use a 5-oz (150-ml) glass.

OLD FASHIONED/ROCKS (5)
Short and wide, heavy-bottomed glass, holding 4–8oz (120–240ml). It is sometimes called a Rocks glass because it is used for serving drinks over ice, or "on the rocks."

PUNCH CUP
Small and rounded with a handle, holding 6–8oz (180–240ml).

SHOT
1-oz (30-ml) glass that can be used for sipping spirits or liqueurs neat or as a 1-oz (30-ml) measuring glass.

WINE (6)
Red wine is traditionally served in a large, bowl-shaped glass, allowing maximum access to oxygen, and therefore maximum flavor and aroma. White, rosé, or sweet dessert wine is served in a smaller, narrower glass that has been chilled.

TYPES OF ICE

Ice and water are the important "weak" parts of your cocktail. Again, we are back to balance. Shaking or stirring your cocktail with ice doesn't just cool the drink—it can leave it consisting of up to 25% water, which is enough to balance out the strong ingredients. The different types of ice you can use serve different purposes, although, to be honest, you could make all the drinks in this book using standard ice cubes from a regular tray.

CLOUDY VS. CLEAR Cloudy ice is perfectly fine, but if you want your cocktails to look extra special, clear ice is the thing. Boil distilled water and let it cool before repeating the process. Pour the cooled water into an ice cube tray and freeze in a closed container, so that the ice doesn't pick up other flavors lurking in the freezer.

ICE CUBES I use ice cubes throughout the book for shaking, stirring, and serving. Larger ice cubes have a slower melting rate, so do a better job of chilling the drink.

CRACKED ICE This is simply ice cubes that have been hit with the back of a barspoon in the palm of your hand, or wrapped in a dishtowel and hammered. You need large sections of ice cube, not crushed ice (see below). The idea is to increase the dilution rate for a drink like an Old Fashioned or a Smash by increasing the amount of surface area of ice in touch with the drink.

CRUSHED ICE This comprises smaller sizes than cracked ice. It's the ice of choice for Juleps and some Mojitos—drinks with a high proportion of strong liquor that needs to be weakened with water. It also weighs down loose ingredients such as mint that you want to keep away from your straw or mouth. You can either buy ready-made crushed ice or wrap ice in a dishtowel and hammer it with a rolling pin, hammer, or other heavy, non-breakable item.

Ice sphere

ICE SPHERE You can now buy ice molds to make large ice spheres, which allow for slower dilution in the glass but for enough water to seep into the spirit to "open" the flavor of the cocktail without making it watery—perfect for an Old Fashioned or a neat drink like a Scotch on the rocks. I use ice spheres filled with a garlic chive flower (see below) to create a flavorsome and attractive garnish in the Bacon and Garlic Old Fashioned (see page 114).

BLOCK ICE This huge block of ice is placed in a punch bowl in order to keep the punch cold without watering it down too much.

EDIBLE FLOWER ICE CUBES Adding edible flowers, berries, or fruit to ice cubes introduces a decorative component and additional flavor. Use double-boiled distilled water that has cooled to half-fill each ice cube mold, then place a flower or berry in the center. Freeze before adding the remaining cooled boiled water up to the rim of the mold. This will ensure your flowers remain in the center of the cube and the cube remains clear. Return the tray to the freezer.

MEASURING

There is a need for accuracy when pouring cocktails if you want to achieve balance and consistency. I have given precise measurements in the recipes but they are not set in stone. If, for example, you prefer a sweeter taste, it's entirely up to you to alter the quantities.

When you come to devise your own cocktail recipes, you may wish to work in "parts," not ounces or milliliters. Simply assign a part to a measurement—for example, 1 part = 1oz (30ml)—then work out the ratios between the different ingredients and take it from there.

MIXING TECHNIQUES

It is easy to work out when to shake, stir, or roll. The end result should be a cocktail that is properly diluted (with ice and water), chilled, and evenly mixed.

DRY SHAKING This is what you do when there are egg whites in a cocktail. It involves shaking the egg white hard without ice for 30 seconds to allow the proteins in the egg white to coagulate and create a foam—they do this more readily when warm, hence the reason for not using ice.

MUDDLING You can use a proper wooden muddler, the disc end of a barspoon, or the end of a wooden spoon to lightly crush fruit or berries in a glass or shaker. The idea is to release the juices. For herbs, it is preferable to "spank" them in the palm of your hands to release the essential oils rather than muddling, which can bruise them and introduce some unwanted bitterness to the drink.

ROLLING This involves chilling a cocktail with minimum dilution and frothing—for example in The Ultimate Bloody Mary (see page 174), where you want to ensure the rich tomato juice isn't watered down or made frothy. Simply pour the mix into a mixing glass or shaker and then immediately "roll," or transfer, the whole mix, including the ice, into another empty mixing glass or shaker. Repeat back and forth between the mixing glasses until your drink is cold. You can then strain as normal into a glass without any ice.

SHAKING Cocktails that include fruit juice, citrus, dairy products, syrups, or thicker liqueurs need to be shaken. Shaking produces a colder drink than stirring and allows for a bit more dilution of water. Put your cocktail

ingredients into your shaker, then fill it two-thirds of the way up with ice cubes. Cover and shake hard for 20 seconds. If the mix contains eggs or cream, you will need to shake for at least 30 seconds.

STERILIZING It is really important, particularly when using organic ingredients, that all jars and bottles are sterilized prior to using them. You can either wash them in really hot, soapy water, and then dry them in an oven at a low temperature, or you can use sterilizing solution/tablets at the prescribed level of dilution to clean them.

STIRRING Cocktails that use spirits only, such as Manhattans and Martinis, should be stirred only. It stops the drink getting cloudy or frothy by introducing less air, and creates a more viscous texture. To stir a cocktail, pour the ingredients in a regular mixing glass or the metal half of a Boston shaker and fill two-thirds of the way up with ice cubes. Use a long-handled barspoon or the handle of a wooden spoon to stir the ingredients for about 20 seconds or until a light frosting appears on the outside of the glass.

GARNISHES

Garnishes are there not just to look pretty; they should provide integral, complementary flavors, aromas, and textures. Throughout the book you will see a selection of shoots, leaves, fronds, and flowers that are used to garnish cocktails. The young leaves and shoots of herbs provide an attractive and more flavorsome garnish than herbs that have flowered. Some leaves, such as scented geranium (see Raspberry and Scented Geranium Sour, pages 140–41), are used on the top of a cocktail for the guest to rub and sniff, releasing aromas that stimulate the appetite.

Edible flowers, fruit, berries, and leaves can also be used throughout the drink, wedged between ice cubes and the glass to create overall visual impact and interest.

APPLE FAN
You can make an attractive fan with apples, strawberries, and other fruits that have a firm enough flesh and skin to hold the shape. Simply halve your fruit and slice very thinly but don't cut to the bottom—leave a tail at the bottom of each piece. Spread the slices out in a fan shape and secure with a toothpick (cocktail stick). Apples need to be soaked in lemon juice if you are preparing them in advance, otherwise they will discolor.

CANDIED CHERRY BLOSSOM
Simply make about ⅓ cup (75ml) of egg wash by mixing 1 lightly whisked egg white and ½ cup (100g) superfine (caster) sugar. Using a fine paintbrush, paint each individual petal on both sides with a light coating of the egg wash and, with your fingers, scatter a light coating of sugar over them before placing on a sheet of parchment paper inside a tray on a sunny windowsill or in a warm area. They may take 24–48 hours to dry. Once dried, store in an airtight container and use within a week. Use for The Cherry Blossom (see page 166).

CANDIED ROSEHIPS Add about ⅔ cup (130g) superfine (caster) sugar, ¼ cup (60ml) water, and 1 cup (250g) rosehips (halved, with their hairy, pithy seeds and membrane removed) into a non-reactive pan. Heat over a medium-high heat until it is boiling vigorously. Tip the rosehips into the pan to coat them and transfer them to parchment paper sprinkled with superfine sugar. Coat them in the sugar and let cool. Once dry, store in an airtight container and use within 2 weeks. Use for the Hedgerow Sour (see page 157).

CITRUS SPIRAL To make lemon spirals (also, confusingly, sometimes called twists), cut the ends of the lemon and make an incision halfway through the lemon lengthwise. Use your thumb to separate the rind from the meat of the lemon until you have removed the whole skin. Roll up the whole skin (including the pith) and cut in pieces to make long, curly twists. Secure the rolls of twists with toothpicks (cocktail sticks) until you need to use them.

CITRUS TWIST A lemon twist, or zest, is an elongated, oval-shaped slice of lemon that you peel off with a vegetable peeler or paring knife. Squeeze the zest over the cocktail, skin side down, to release the essential oils. You can set fire to the oil by holding a match in one hand and zest in the other. Finish by wiping the zest around the rim of the glass and dropping in the drink, to add a wonderful flavor and aroma.

SALT OR SUGAR RIMS These can be used sparingly to give a savory (see Salad Days, page 138), or sweet (see The Cherry Blossom, page 166), touch to a cocktail. Sugars and salts can be smoked or flavored with crushed dried flowers or spices. I use a range of pink and black salts, and flavored sugars. The trick is to make sure the individual crystals are small enough to coat the rim. Use a mortar and pestle to reduce the particle size if you need to.

To add a salt rim, cut a slot into a wedge of citrus and gently rub it around the rim of the glass. I prefer to coat only half the rim so guests can choose whether or not to drink from that side. Hold the glass tilted sideways and dab a section of the rim in a saucer of salt, slowly turning the glass so that only the outer edge is coated. Shake off the excess. For a sweet cocktail, do the same with the glass in a saucer of simple or flavored syrup.

EXPERIMENTAL MIXOLOGY ON A BUDGET

Gastronomy and science have encroached into drinks' territory with incredible results. You can play around with taste, smell, and texture with all manner of foams, infusion techniques, and smoke. Like any hobby or pastime, cocktail mixology can all too easily become a money pit the deeper you delve into it—the gadgets of professional pioneers and geeks in this world are fancy and expensive. However, with a bit of ingenuity and just a couple of indulgences, you, too, can have some fun experimenting.

FOAMS

Essentially, foams create a beautiful mouth-feel. They provide contrast and smooth out other elements of the drink. For example, a Sour would just be a tart drink but if it is made with egg white, you can create a layer of decadent creaminess that transforms it. Foams also provide a perfect surface on which to rest your edible garnish or bitters.

Foams are made by trapping air or gas bubbles in either a liquid or solid substance, while allowing both of these to become stable. We use egg white, cream, coconut milk, or gelatin (or vegetarian equivalent) to create a protein-fat combination that provides this stability. When liquefied and charged with air or gas bubbles, they create a silky, creamy foam.

EGG WHITE FOAM
Egg whites on their own will create a thin, flavorless, but very stable layer of foam. The great thing about them is that they don't taste of anything and, when combined with citrus and sugar, they create a great texture, as well as unifying the flavors. A good point to note is the fresher the egg, the more stable the foam—it's something to do with the strengths of the protein in the albumen.

Add ½oz (15ml) of egg white per cocktail (a large egg is about 1oz/30ml) to a cocktail shaker, together with your other ingredients, except ice, cover it, and dry-shake (see page 33) vigorously for 30 seconds. Once the egg is emulsified, add the ice cubes to the shaker as normal and shake for another 20 seconds to properly chill your drink. Strain and pour into the prepared cocktail glass. Wait a few seconds for the foam to settle down before adding your choice of garnish.

GELATIN FOAM
Foams can also add another integral layer of flavor if they include juices, spirits, liqueurs, or cream alongside a protein-fat combination like egg white or cream. Gelatin is a protein that creates a thicker, denser foam than egg white, but egg white is a better stabilizer of foam than gelatin, so for this foam I use both. Importantly, I also use a professional cream whipper (available from quality catering suppliers), with nitrous oxide (N_2O) to charge the foam with air and work its magic. You could use a hand or electric blender instead, but you will be there a very long time and the whipper provides the perfect dispenser to serve the foam on top of the drink.

You will need to experiment with ingredients but, as a guide, work on the basis of 12oz (360ml) of a base comprising juice/syrup/liqueur (you need a balance of acid and sweet) with an additional 4oz (120ml) egg white and 1–2 sheets of gelatin. These clear sheets need to be "bloomed," or made pliable, in iced water to create a liquid gel.

It is very important when using a professional whipper that the liquid you pour into the whipper is free of particles, because it will easily clog otherwise. Use a sieve for straining any liquid you pour in. Remember that foams will stabilize after they have been charged if left for at least 4 hours in the refrigerator. Always refrigerate your whipper between uses, and shake well each time before using. If your foam is too thick, use less gelatin another time. If it is too runny, add more gelatin. Juice-based foams can last up to a week. Foams containing alcohol should be consumed within 3 days.

ROWAN, HONEY, AND LEMON FOAM

This recipe for a gelatin-based foam is used in The Honeysuckle (see page 180). The Rowan Syrup (see page 92) works beautifully with the brandy, while the honey and lemon create a perfect sweet/sour balance to the whole drink.

1½ sheets gelatin (platinum grade)

2oz (60ml) runny honey

2oz (60ml) Rowan Syrup (see page 92)

2oz (60ml) lemon juice

6oz (180ml) hot water

4oz (120ml) pasteurized egg whites

Wild honeysuckle blossom

Professional cream whipper with 2 N2O cartridges

Makes enough foam for 15 drinks

Place the gelatin sheets in a bowl of iced water and soak them until they are pliable (about 10 minutes). Meanwhile, combine the honey, Rowan Syrup, lemon juice, and hot water in a nonreactive pan over a very low heat, until the honey is dissolved. Strain using a fine-mesh sieve into a clean pan.

Squeeze the excess water from the softened gelatin sheets. Drop the sheets into the pan containing the mix and heat gently to dissolve the gelatin. Stir constantly and do not allow to reach boiling point. Turn off the heat as soon as the gelatin is dissolved. Let cool to room temperature (about 15 minutes).

Place the egg whites in a bowl and lightly whisk with a fork or whisk until slightly frothy and pour into the pan. Funnel this liquid into the whipper. Charge it with the 2 N2O cartridges, following the manufacturer's instructions. Shake well for at least a minute and refrigerate. Let the foam stabilize for a minimum of 2 hours, preferably overnight, before using.

Shake the whipper well before dispensing. Tip it upside down so that it is completely inverted over the cocktail. Let the foam settle for 20 seconds before garnishing with wild honeysuckle blossom.

Honeysuckle

STRAWBERRY AND CREAM FOAM

This is essentially a strawberry-flavored whipped cream for the Limoncello with Strawberries and Cream Foam (see page 120) but I have used some additional gelatin and charged it with nitrous oxide to create a denser, stable foam.

1¼ sheets gelatin (platinum grade)

6oz (180g) strawberries, hulled

2oz (60ml) freshly squeezed lemon juice

3oz (90ml) Simple Syrup (see page 68)

2oz (60ml) hot water

⅓ cup (80ml) heavy (double) cream

Professional cream whipper with 2 N2O cartridges

Makes enough foam for 15 drinks

Place the gelatin sheets in a bowl of iced water to soak until they are pliable (about 10 minutes). Meanwhile, blend the strawberries and lemon juice on a high speed until smooth, and strain through a fine-mesh sieve into a small pan. Add the Simple Syrup and hot water, and stir on a low heat to combine all the ingredients.

Squeeze the excess water from the softened gelatin sheets, drop them into the pan containing the mix, and heat gently to dissolve the gelatin. Stir constantly and do not allow to reach boiling point. Turn off the heat as soon as the gelatin has dissolved. Let cool to room temperature (about 15 minutes).

Add the cream to the mix and funnel through a sieve into the whipper. Charge it with the 2 N2O cartridges, following the manufacturer's instructions. Shake well for at least a minute and refrigerate for a minimum of 2 hours, preferably overnight, before using.

Shake the whipper well before dispensing. Tip it upside down so that it is completely inverted over the cocktail.

FAT WASHING

The world of savory cocktails is awash, quite literally, with all manner of fatty ingredients. Fat washing is a very easy way to infuse spirits with flavorsome fattiness, whether it's smoked bacon, peanut butter, or almonds. The Bacon and Tea, Smoke-infused Whisky recipe opposite combines this technique with some good, ole-fashioned smokin'...

SMOKING

While it's unnecessary to smoke a really good single malt whisky that already has a substantial peat-based smokiness, other whiskies, such as bourbon, do have a natural affinity with smoke that works very well in cocktails.

It's important not to over-smoke a cocktail, but this is, unfortunately, very easy to do and creates a world of unpleasantness. You will need a reasonably inexpensive hand-held smoker and then you can experiment with the ingredients you would like to smoke. Different kinds of wood chip come supplied with the smoker kit but you can try out loose-leaf smoky teas like Lagsang Souchong, as I have opposite, or Orange Blossom Oolong tea, or even dried flowers.

You can also use your hand-held smoker to smoke some sugar or salt for a cocktail rim or even smoke your sugar prior to adding it to a pan to make a sugar syrup with an essence of smokiness.

BACON AND TEA, SMOKE-INFUSED WHISKY

This recipe combines a fat washing infusion and some smoking—perfect for a Bacon and Garlic Old Fashioned (see page 114).

1 pound (450g) thick, fatty, smoked bacon

700 or 750ml bottle of blended Scotch whisky

1 tsp loose-leaf Lapsang Souchong tea

2 x 1-quart (1-liter) freezer-safe, wide-mouthed, sealable jars, sterilized (see page 33)

Hand-held smoker kit

Sealable presentation bottle(s), sterilized (see page 33)

Makes approximately 1½ pints (750ml)

Warm a skillet (frying pan) and add the bacon, sautéeing on a medium heat until cooked but not burnt. Drain off the bacon fat into a wide-mouthed pitcher, then strain the mix into one of the jars to remove any pieces of bacon. Add the whisky. Seal and shake vigorously to combine and let sit for at least 2 hours to infuse and allow the fat particles to rise to the surface.

Place the jar in the freezer overnight to solidify the fat. Use a spoon to remove the solid fat, then strain the unfrozen bacon-washed whisky underneath into the second jar. Either funnel the whisky into a sterilized presentation bottle or store the jar in a freezer or dark place. As fat has the capacity to go rancid after time, this infusion is best consumed within a month.

Do the following only immediately prior to serving your cocktail, so that none of the smokiness is lost. Add your chosen smoking ingredient to the smoker—I used Lapsang Souchong tea mixed with some apple and hickory wood chips.

Light the smoker and hold the pipe just inside the jar, with a clean dishtowel over the opening to prevent the smoke escaping. As soon as the jar starts to fill up with smoke, remove the pipe, put on the lid, and turn off the gun. Shake the jar, funnel the whisky into a presentation bottle, then pour into your chosen cocktail.

Mezcal, which is made in Mexico by smoking the hearts of the agave plant (see page 18), is another strong candidate for smoking. Use it in this recipe instead of Scotch for an interesting and delicious alternative.

CHAPTER 2

COCKTAIL ELEMENTS

There are four main elements that can be included in a cocktail: the strong (alcoholic spirits); the sweet (sugar or its equivalent natural sweetener, such as fresh fruit or plants); the bitter (herbs, spices, bark, roots, or peel); and the acid (citrus fruit but also occasionally milk, tree fruit, wine, or vinegar). In addition, there are two other, more minor elements: the weak (ice, water, or soda water) and the mild or smooth (eggs or cream), which I've talked about on page 36.

The first cocktails were simply a mix of spirit, sugar, water (which could be ice), and bitters, but tastes have changed over time. The modern palate tends to enjoy a balance of sweet and sour, although many people don't like sweet cocktails at all and head straight for a dry, aromatic drink, such as a Martini (spirit plus a bitter, aromatized wine) or a sour drink made with a base spirit, citrus, and a small amount of sugar, sometimes with egg white or cream to smooth it out and provide a pleasant mouth-feel. Whatever the personal preference, balance is the key to a good drink, and you will see from the following recipes that by combining strong, sweet, acid, and bitter you can create harmony and joy in a glass!

THE STRONG

There is a rule of thumb that if the primary sense triggered by an ingredient is smell, as with lavender, the best way to extract it is by making an infusion in alcohol. If, on the other hand, the ingredient doesn't smell particularly but has a strong flavor, like raspberries, you will achieve the best result by combining it with a sweetener and water in a syrup. For an ingredient that scores highly on flavor as well as smell, such as lemons, you can get maximum results by performing both operations and making a liqueur, which is an alcoholic infusion with sugar added later.

INFUSIONS AND MACERATIONS

Cocktail mixologists, herbalists, tea-makers, and pharmacists will all provide conflicting definitions of infusions and macerations. For the purposes of this book, though, infusion is the catch-all phrase to describe the extraction of flavor, color, vitamins, and other constituent parts of a leaf, flower, root, citrus peel, and so on, into a solvent, such as alcohol, water, oil, or vinegar. It can be a hot or cold process.

That said, I tend to use the term "infusion" here for a rapid heat process, and "maceration" for a cold one. Although maceration can take longer, the results are usually better. Fruit is particularly suited to this process and can be macerated in alcohol, sugar, citrus, or vinegar. When fruit or certain petals are combined with sugar and placed in a dark environment at room temperature, the sugar absorbs the color, flavor, and moisture of whatever it has been placed with and some kind of alchemy takes place. There's not the space here, nor do I have the scientific background, to explain this properly, but after 24–48 hours you will end up with a small quantity of bright and clear liquid.

As with most things, there is a huge number of ways to infuse, but a few rules of thumb will keep things reasonably simple. I would suggest using a high-proof/alcohol by volume (ABV)—80 proof/40% ABV spirit, or higher—where possible. This will extract the maximum amount of flavor and herbal alkaloids from your ingredients, and the high-alcohol content will act as a preservative, increasing the shelf life of your infusion. Most people start infusing with vodka, which has a neutral taste, before getting more adventurous with other flavor combinations.

Less is usually more in terms of time when infusing herbs. Most herbs, including fennel, rosemary, lavender, and lemon balm, take a very short time (sometimes just a few hours) to infuse. And once they're done, they're done. Any longer and the flavor moves quickly from intense to bitter. This actually applies to all ingredients, but particularly to herbs. Leaving organic plant matter in liquid, even if this is alcohol, will only cause unpleasantness in the long term. While I would urge experimentation, provided it is accompanied by frequent tasting, a general guide for infusion times is as follows:

- **Strong flavors like lavender, vanilla beans (pods), or hot peppers: anything from a couple of hours to a day.**

- **Fresh herbs, citrus zest, pine needles, fresh ginger: one to three days maximum.**

- **Most stone fruits, berries: three days to a week (sloes, for example, take much longer)**

- **Vegetables, apples, pears: five to seven days.**

- **Dried spices and really mild flavors, like nuts: up to two weeks.**

As for quantities, use half the amount of dried herbs as you would fresh, and work on the basis of the following ratios with your chosen spirit. Of course, there are many exceptions to any rule but if you follow these guidelines, you can't go too badly wrong.

- **Fresh herbs, citrus zest, pine needles, fresh ginger: 1:4 ingredient to spirit**

- **Dried herbs: 1:8 ingredient to spirit**

- **Berries, fruits, stone fruits, tree fruit, vegetables: 1:1 ingredient to spirit**

- **Dried spices: 1:10 ingredient to spirit**

Horseradish and BLACK CARDAMOM VODKA

This infusion is the perfect base for the Ultimate Bloody Mary (see page 174), and the horseradish can take less than an hour to infuse if you use a very fine zester, such as a Microplane. The smokiness in the black cardamom is created by drying the pods over open flames, which is the traditional method used on the Indian sub-continent. This blends wonderfully with the mustard oil released by grating the fresh horseradish root. What more could you want on a cold bonfire night than heat and smokiness?

3-in (7.5-cm) length of horseradish root

700 or 750ml bottle of vodka, 80 proof/40% ABV

4 black cardamom pods

1-quart (1-liter) wide-mouthed, sealable jar, sterilized (see page 33)

Sealable presentation bottle(s), sterilized (see page 33)

Makes approximately 1½ pints (750ml)

Wash, peel, and loosely grate the horseradish root until you have 1 cupful. Combine with the vodka in the sterilized jar.

Crack the black cardamom pods with a mortar and pestle, and add to the vodka and horseradish. Seal the jar and leave in a cool, dark place for about 5 days, upending the jar gently a couple of times once a day. While the horseradish only takes about an hour to infuse if grated with a Microplane zester, as opposed to a few days if you were to chop it coarsely, the dried cardamom really needs about 5 days to marry with the horseradish and release the desired taste into the vodka.

Strain the infusion into a wide-mouthed pitcher, then funnel it into the sterilized presentation bottle(s) and seal. Keep in the freezer or a dark place for up to a year.

> You can grow horseradish yourself in a deep pot or a patch of ground, where it will happily colonize anything else you've got growing there! You can also find it growing wild in parks and woodland, and near marshes, but it is important to note it's illegal to pick anything by its root.

WILD CHERRY-INFUSED
Rye Whiskey

A high-proof rye offers spiciness, fruitiness, and natural bitterness, and the high-alcohol content extracts as much of the cherry flavor as possible. No sugar is added to this beautiful infusion, which creates the perfect balance with the sweet complexity of the Carpano Antica vermouth used in a Wild Cherry Manhattan (see page 162).

2 cups (500g) wild cherries (store-bought cherries are also fine but they are likely to be a lot sweeter)

700 or 750ml bottle of rye whiskey, 80 proof/40% ABV, such as Rittenhouse Straight Rye

1-quart (1-liter) wide-mouthed, sealable jar, sterilized (see page 33)

Makes approximately 1½ pints (750ml)

Wash and score the cherries with a knife (there's no need to take the pits/stones out, as they add a small and pleasant amount of bitterness over time). Place in the sterilized jar. Pour the rye whiskey over the cherries, making sure they are all covered. Seal the jar and store in a cool, dry place. And wait. Once a week, upend the jar slowly a couple of times.

The infusion will be very drinkable after a month, and even better after two. It is up to you whether you strain it before drinking, but after 3 months, you should definitely do so (see page 26) and funnel it into a clean jar to remove the cherries.

Use the whiskey-soaked cherries as a garnish or in ice cream. Once you've tasted these, you will forever recoil at the sight of a store-bought, glow-in-the-dark maraschino cherry.

Foraged cherries could be either *Prunus avium* (sweet or wild cherry) or *P. cerasus* (sour or morello cherry, which is dark red, and amarelle, which is lighter). Growing in parks, woodland areas, and hedgerows, they are best picked when they are as dark and, therefore, as sweet as possible, but obviously before the birds have got to them. Sour cherries and their crushed pips are used as the base for maraschino liqueur, so if you use them here, you will get hints of that glorious flavor.

Rose petal VODKA

This infusion is quite subtle and delicious. I took a tip from Liz Knight of Forage Fine Foods in Herefordshire, U.K., who makes the most exquisite rose petal syrup. She snips off the bitter white bits at the bottom of each petal. I also only pick the petals, rather than the central flower, as I want to be able to come back later in the year to pick the rosehips.

Enough rose petals to fill the jar loosely

700 or 750ml bottle of vodka, 80 proof/40% ABV

2 tbsp (25g) superfine (caster) sugar, to taste

1-quart (1-liter) wide-mouthed, sealable jar, sterilized (see page 33)

Sealable presentation bottle(s), sterilized (see page 33)

Makes approximately 1½ pints (750ml)

Pick over the rose petals to remove any wildlife, but do not wash them. Loosely pack them into the jar. Pour the vodka up to the very top of the jar to ensure there is no air. Leave for 24 hours and taste—it will be ready when there is an earthy, pungent scent of roses. The taste deteriorates after the third day, so check regularly.

Strain the infusion into a wide-mouthed pitcher. Clean and dry the jar. Pour the infusion back into it. Add sugar to taste. It's better to err on the less sweet side, as you can always add a sweetener (see pages 68–69) to your cocktails later. Once ready, use a funnel to pour into the sterilized presentation bottle(s) and seal. Store in a cool, dark place and use within 6 months.

ROSE PETAL GIN

Gin makes a delicious alternative to vodka in this recipe, but I would urge you to use a gin that contains only a few botanicals to reduce the chance of your rose petals clashing with other flavors.

The type of rose you use depends on what's around. *Rosa rugosa* is very common in the U.K. in municipal sites and private gardens, and has a beautiful aroma and color. Slightly more delicate, though equally delicious, is *R. canina*, the wild dog rose, which can be found romping through hedgerows and parks. For aesthetic reasons, I generally add a few crimson petals when using dog roses to give some added color to the vodka.

It's a good idea to collect only the freshest, newly opened roses and to do so early in the morning after a spell of good sunshine and warmth. Without that, they often lack the desired scent.

Lavender GIN

English lavender (*Lavandula angustifolia*) is the most fragrant and, therefore, the perfect type of lavender for this recipe. I particularly like the cultivar 'Munstead'. If you can't find that, *L. × intermedia* 'Provence' (French lavender) has a milder, sweeter flavor, which is also good. Lavender is particularly potent, so to stop the infusion smelling like an old underwear drawer, use it sparingly, and only infuse it for a very short time, otherwise a nasty bitterness will pervade. But, get the balance right and you'll have floral notes singing beautifully in a wide variety of summer cocktails.

Harvest fresh, unsprayed lavender when the flowers have been exposed to plenty of sun, so that as much essential oil is produced as possible. The flowers should be showing signs of purple but not be fully open.

Remember that the potency of herbs increases with drying, so use a third of the quantity of culinary-grade dried flowers to fresh.

6 tsp fresh lavender blossoms or 2 tsp dried, fragrant, culinary-grade lavender

1 liter bottle of floral gin, such as Jensen Old Tom

1-quart (1-liter) wide-mouthed, sealable jar, sterilized (see page 33)

Sealable presentation bottle(s), sterilized (see page 33)

Makes approximately 1 quart (1 liter)

Place the fresh or dried lavender blossoms in the jar. Pour in the gin. Seal the jar, upend it gently a couple of times, and place somewhere dark at room temperature. Leave for 5–8 hours, testing after 5 hours, then every hour to make sure there is no bitterness emerging. (To speed things up, heat the lavender gently in a pan with half the gin. As soon as it reaches boiling point, take off the heat, let cool, and add the remaining gin.)

Strain the infusion into the sterilized presentation bottle(s), seal, and store in a cool, dark place. Both methods will result in a gin with a pinkish-purple hue.

WILD FENNEL, FIG, GRILLED BERGAMOT, *and Star Anise Rum*

What we have here is a heady and extravagant mélange that will have you purring. I wanted the natural sweetness of a good white rum to balance the spiciness, sourness, and sweetness from the strong and complex flavors of fennel, figs, bergamots, and star anise—not a dark rum that would mask them.

2 x bergamots

Demerara/turbinado sugar, for dipping bergamot slices

2 cups (300g) fresh figs, quartered

1⅓ cups (200g) dried figs, sliced

4 x 8-in (20-cm) long stalks of wild fennel fronds or 1 fennel bulb, sliced into 1-in (2.5-cm) pieces

6 star anise

1 liter bottle of good-quality white rum

1-quart (1-liter) wide-mouthed, sealable jar, sterilized (see page 33)

Makes approximately 1 quart (1 liter)

Slice one of the bergamots, dip one cut side of each slice in the sugar, and grill over a high heat on a grill (barbecue) or in a skillet (frying pan) for 30 seconds until charred and beginning to caramelize. Repeat for the other side of the slices. Place them in the jar.

Peel the zest of the other bergamot with a vegetable peeler (not a grater), avoiding the white pith, and place in the jar. Add the remaining ingredients, making sure they are all covered by the rum. The figs will absorb liquid as they infuse, so there needs to be enough liquid to prevent them from poking out of the infusion after a couple of days. Seal the jar, upend gently a couple of times, and place in the refrigerator.

As there is citrus in this infusion, you really need to check your jar daily for taste and appearance. The grilled bergamot wheels definitely need to come out after 3 days to avoid the risk of them going bad. The other ingredients can remain for up to a week, but remove the bergamot rind as soon as it has gone hard.

Once the infusion is complete, strain and funnel into the sterilized presentation bottle(s) and seal. Store in a cool, dark place and consume within 6 months.

Bergamot (*Citrus bergamia*), the small, exotic, sour orange fruit used in perfumes and Earl Grey tea, has an exceptional flavor, somewhere between that of an orange and a lemon—but that description does not do it justice. It's more floral than lemon, and I am using it here more as a spice. I wanted the charred, smoky sourness and caramel sweetness from the grilled bergamot flesh, but I've also added some plain bergamot peel for its essential oils and fragrance.

The complexity and depth of flavor in dried figs led me to add a few to the fresh ones, but it's not absolutely necessary.

Cacao Nib VODKA

I wouldn't recommend drinking this on its own, but it works very well as a float in the adulterated version of a Chocolate Mint Julep (see page 115). You can also use the nibs as a chocolate rim on glasses for dessert cocktails. They are available from health food stores and artisanal chocolate manufacturers.

Cacao nibs are essentially raw chocolate—pieces of cacao beans that have been roasted, hulled, and prepared before the stage of actually making chocolate. They taste slightly more of roasted coffee beans, although you can detect chocolate, and give a very pleasing, grown-up bitter chocolate note to drinks.

7oz (200g) roasted cacao nibs
700 or 750ml bottle of 80 proof/ 40% ABV vodka

1-quart (1-liter) wide-mouthed, sealable jar, sterilized (see page 33)
Sealable presentation bottle(s), sterilized (see page 33)

Makes approximately 1½ pints (750ml)

Place the roasted cacao nibs in the sealable jar and pour the vodka over them. Seal the jar and upend it gently a couple of times. Store in a cool, dark place for 2–3 days, but no longer. Taste each day and when you have the desired combination of bitterness and chocolate, strain the liquid into a wide-mouthed pitcher, then funnel into the presentation bottle(s). It will be an amber, reddish color, very dry, and very grown up.

False ACACIA GIN

I have three huge false acacia or black locust (*Robinia pseudoacacia*) trees on the terrace outside Midnight Apothecary. In late spring, they are laden with huge heads of fragrant, white blossoms. I simply infuse them in gin and use in Martinis to provide honey notes without the cloying sweetness. Label this infusion "Black Locust Gin" if you want to scare your guests!

6 heads of false acacia blossoms
1 liter bottle of gin, 80 proof/40% ABV

1-quart (1-liter) wide-mouthed, sealable jar, sterilized (see page 33)
Sealable presentation bottle(s), sterilized (see page 33)

Makes approximately 1 quart (1 liter)

Shake the blossom heads free of wildlife and cut off any stems or greenery. Place the individual unwashed blossoms in the jar and pour over the gin. Seal, shake gently, and keep in a cool, dark place. Taste after the second day—I usually find the infusion is ready after about 4 days. Strain the infusion into a wide-mouthed pitcher, then funnel into the sterilized presentation bottle(s) and seal. Store in a cool, dark place and consume within 6 months.

Scented Geranium VODKA

Scented geraniums (*Pelargonium*) are a fantastic aromatic and visual addition to gardens and cocktails. The leaves can be rubbed and sniffed as an appetite-stimulating garnish on a foam, such as Raspberry and Scented Geranium Sour (see page 140), or the leaves can be infused in a spirit or syrup. The flowers, too, make an attractive garnish, with a faint citrus flavor.

2 large handfuls of unsprayed rose-scented geranium leaves, such as *Pelargonium graveolens* or *P.* 'Attar of Roses'

700 or 750ml bottle of vodka, 80 proof/40% ABV

1-quart (1-liter) wide-mouthed, sealable jar, sterilized (see page 33)

Sealable presentation bottle(s), sterilized (see page 33)

Makes approximately 1½ pints (750ml)

Smack the individual unwashed leaves between your hands to release the essential oil before dropping them into the jar. Cover with the vodka. Seal and upend the jar gently a couple of times. Leave in a cool, dark place for 24 hours.

Taste to see if you are getting a strong flavor of scented geranium. If you aren't, reseal and leave for a maximum of 48 hours. Strain the infusion into a wide-mouthed pitcher, then funnel into the sterilized presentation bottle(s) and seal. Store in a cool, dark place and use within 6 months.

> There are many differently scented geraniums, but I would recommend a citrus one, such as *Pelargonium* 'Lemon Fancy' or the rose-scented *P. graveolens*, which is also surprisingly sweet. While others smell of anything from chocolate, peppermint, and nutmeg to oranges, strawberries, and coconut, they often taste too vegetal.

Douglas Fir VODKA

This forms the basis of the Woodland Martini (see page 170). I have used a neutral-tasting spirit—vodka—as I wanted the clean, lemony, piny scent of the Douglas fir to shine through. This recipe is designed to be drunk with your eyes closed to conjure up a woodland walk.

3 handfuls of young Douglas fir needles

2 x 2-in (5-cm) lengths of very thin, woody Douglas fir stems

700 or 750ml bottle of vodka, 80 proof/40% ABV

1-quart (1-liter) wide-mouthed, sealable jar, sterilized (see page 33)

Sealable presentation bottle(s), sterilized (see page 33)

Makes approximately 1½ pints (750ml)

Place the Douglas fir needles and woody stems in a blender, adding enough vodka to cover, and blend for at least 30 seconds on a high speed.

Pour the bright green mix into the jar and add the remaining vodka. Seal, upend gently a couple of times, and store in a cool, dark place. Upend daily and start tasting after the second day. This infusion should take no longer than 4 days to work its magic—you want the lemon and pine notes of woodland, not a bathroom cleaner. Strain the infusion into a wide-mouthed pitcher when you think you're there, then funnel into the sterilized presentation bottle(s) and seal. Store in a cool, dark place and consume within 6 months.

FENNEL-INFUSED GIN OR VODKA

I'm putting this simple recipe here for no other reason than the infusion time for the fennel is roughly the same as that for the Douglas fir needles. Clean and finely slice one small fennel bulb and add to a 700 or 750ml bottle of 80 proof/40% ABV gin or vodka. Follow the same protocol as above. The infusion should be ready after 5 days at the most.

> If you use your thumbnail or a knife to cut into the very young woody stems of Douglas fir, you will get an overwhelming lemony scent, so a couple of inches of stem is good added to this mix. Any more, though, and it will become overpoweringly bitter.

Gold rum is a good halfway house in terms of flavor and price, but if you are feeling flush, splash out on a good-quality *rhum agricole* (agricultural rum) from Martinique. Made exclusively from sugarcane juice, it is almost clear and bursting with natural flavor.

★

Once your infusion is ready, a fresh nasturtium flower will look stunning in the finished cocktail and, if you eat the whole blossom, you'll get the sweetness of the nectar alongside the spiciness of the pepper (see Nasturtium Collins, page 144). The leaves are also deliciously peppery.

Nasturtium RUM

Many flowers look fantastic but taste insipid. However, nasturtiums are bold in appearance as well as flavor. The sweetness of the molasses or sugarcane juice in rum needs a punchy, spicy flavor to team up with, and the pepperiness of nasturtium is ideal.

Enough nasturtium flowers (about 40) to fill the jar loosely

1 liter bottle of golden rum, 80 proof/40% ABV

1-quart (1-liter) wide-mouthed, sealable jar, sterilized (see page 33)

Sealable presentation bottle(s), sterilized (see page 33)

Makes approximately 1½ pints (750ml)

Pick over the nasturtium flowers and remove any wildlife. Pack the unwashed blossoms gently into the jar and pour the rum over the top, making sure the flowers are completely covered. Seal the jar, upend it gently a couple of times, and leave in a cool, dark place. The pepperiness takes a while to really work in this infusion, so check after 7 days and wait a maximum of 3 weeks—certainly no longer.

Strain the infusion into a wide-mouthed pitcher, then funnel into the sterilized presentation bottle(s) and seal. Store in a cool, dark place and consume within 6 months.

OTHER NASTURTIUM INFUSIONS

Use tequila, gin, or vodka in place of the rum.

LIQUEURS

Liqueurs, which can be savored on their own or used to complement other strong spirits, provide the essential "strong and sweet" element present in many cocktails. They are perfect for capturing the taste as well as the scent of those ingredients that score highly in both categories.

A liqueur is simply a distilled spirit to which your chosen fruit/blossom/herb/spice has been added, together with some sugar. Whether you macerate the solid ingredients in the spirit first and then add the sugar later, or put in everything together, is up to you. I prefer to make a liqueur in two stages for two reasons: the maximum flavor is extracted from the solid ingredient in the high-proof alcohol first and, most important, the taste can be adjusted for the desired level of sweetness once this has been done, giving you more control over the maceration process. You will see in the following pages though, that, as always, there are exceptions!

Elderflower LIQUEUR

This is another case of cocktail alchemy. The common, workhorse shrub elderberry (*Sambucus nigra*), which grows in towns and rural areas alike, produces a variety of almost year-round ingredients. The elderflowers signal the start of summer and produce a very floral, elegant liqueur, perfect for a Chelsea Fringe Collins (see page 116).

20 large elderflower heads
½ cup (100g) superfine (caster) sugar
**1 liter bottle of vodka,
80 proof/40% ABV**
**1 unwaxed, organic lemon (see
page 15), thinly sliced**

**1-quart (1-liter) wide-mouthed,
sealable jar, sterilized (see page 33)**
**Sealable presentation bottle(s),
sterilized (see page 33)**

Makes approximately 1 quart (1 liter)

Shake the elderflower heads free of unwanted wildlife but do not wash them. Remove all the leaves and as many stalks as you can, as these are slightly toxic (the very tiny stalks that are attached to each flower are fine).

Place the flowers in the sterilized jar and compress slightly with your hand. Add the sugar, followed by the vodka—adding the sugar at this stage helps to draw out the flavor of the elderflowers. Place the lemon slices on top of the flowers to weigh them down—you really don't want the flowers to oxidize by rising above the surface of the alcohol. If the lemon slices don't do the trick, add a small plate or a lid that fits snugly in the jar.

Seal the jar and store in a cool, dark place for a month. Upend it gently a couple of times during the month, to make sure the sugar has dissolved. After 1 month, strain the liquid twice into a wide-mouthed pitcher, first through a fine-mesh strainer to remove the flower debris, then through a coffee filter or several layers of cheesecloth to catch the minute particles, so that the liqueur is not cloudy. Store somewhere cool and dark. Once opened, keep in the refrigerator and consume within 6 months.

To avoid making something akin to what the local tomcat produces to mark out its territory, use only big, full elderflower heads that are almost brilliant white and have been in direct sun—even one brown flower can negatively affect the flavor. They should also smell wonderful, so trust your nose.

Pick the flowers before noon, as the aroma fades after that, and hurry home to make your liqueur within one or two hours of picking because the perfume and subsequent flavor really do fade fast.

Scented Geranium and Lavender LIMONCELLO

Limoncello is a taste of lemony sunshine and could be left without any adornment, but I just wanted to experiment with a couple of flavors to see if things improved. I think they did—this recipe is utterly delicious and super-easy to make. If you are a believer in "more is more," then it makes a great base for the Limoncello with Strawberries and Cream Foam (see page 120). Please note that this recipe is made over the course of a month, so you will not need all the ingredients at the start.

Zest of 10 large, unwaxed, organic lemons (see page 15), without any white pith

700 or 750ml bottle of vodka, 80 proof/40% ABV or above, or pure grain alcohol

10 scented geranium (*Pelargonium*) leaves

1 tbsp culinary-grade lavender buds

1 cup (250ml) water if using 80 proof/40% ABV vodka; 3 cups (750ml) water if using 100 proof/50% ABV (or above) vodka

2 cups (400g) superfine (caster) sugar

1-quart (1-liter) wide-mouthed, sealable jar, sterilized (see page 33)

Sealable presentation bottle(s), sterilized (see page 33)

Makes approximately 1 quart (1 liter)

Pour the zest into the sterilized jar, followed by the alcohol. Seal the jar, shake, and leave in a cool, dark place for a month, upending gently a couple of times a week.

Five days before the month is up, smack the individual scented geranium leaves between your palms, to release the essential oils, and drop into the jar. Add the lavender as well. Seal the jar and upend it gently a couple of times.

Prepare a simple syrup by heating the water (see note in the Ingredients list about the quantity of water in relation to the strength of vodka) and sugar in a nonreactive pan, stirring to dissolve the sugar. Once it has reached boiling point, remove from the heat and let cool.

Strain the alcohol into a wide-mouthed pitcher and add the syrup. Stir, then funnel into the sterilized presentation bottle(s). Seal. You can store limoncello in the freezer or somewhere dark for up to a year. It is best to leave it for another 2 weeks, at the very least, and longer if you have the patience because it will become smoother with age.

ARANCELLO

To make this delicious blood orange liqueur, simply substitute the zest of blood oranges for the lemons, and follow the same directions.

Ideally, use sweet Meyer lemons, but if you can't get them, unwaxed, organic ones will do. You should get equally delicious results experimenting with other types of citrus too. A high-proof alcohol (at least 80 proof/40% ABV) will give as much flavor as possible to the infusion.

Proper Italian limoncello is simply vodka with lemon peel and sugar—nature does the rest. The cheap, angry liquid that you are sometimes served as a complimentary digestif in a restaurant should not put you off the real thing.

A very fine zester, such as a Microplane (see page 27), makes the job so much quicker and ensures you don't include any bitter pith in the infusion.

NOCINO

This spicy, sweet, nutty, earthy, slightly bitter liqueur is made with unripe, soft green walnuts, still in their green husks. There's a walnut tree (*Juglans regia*) growing close to my home, which is lucky because it's rare to find green walnuts for sale. It's gorgeous drunk on its own or in Manhattans, Sidecars, Negronis, and Nocino Nights (see page 179).

25 green walnuts with soft husks

Zest of 1 unwaxed, organic lemon (see page 15), peeled with the vegetable peeler

1 cinnamon stick

5 whole cloves

700 or 750ml bottle of high-proof (preferably 100 proof/50% ABV) vodka or other grain spirit

1 cup (200g) superfine (caster) sugar

1 cup (250ml) water

1-quart (1-liter) wide-mouthed, sealable jar, sterilized (see page 33)

Sealable presentation bottle(s), sterilized (see page 33)

Makes approximately 1½ pints (750ml)

Wash and wipe the green walnuts dry with a dishtowel. Wearing gloves and using a nonabsorbent chopping board, quarter the walnuts carefully with a sharp, heavy knife. Add them to the sterilized jar, together with the peeled lemon zest, cinnamon stick, and cloves. Pour the vodka (or other grain spirit) over the ingredients, making sure they are all covered. Seal the jar, upend it gently a couple of times, and store in a cool, dark place for 40 days, upending the jar a couple of times a week. Strain the black liquid into a wide-mouthed pitcher.

To make the simple syrup, place the sugar and water in a nonreactive pan and heat gently, stirring occasionally, until the sugar has dissolved. Add the syrup to the wide-mouthed pitcher, then pour the walnut and syrup mix into the cleaned jar. Upend the jar gently a couple of times, then store in a cool, dark place for another 40 days.

Funnel the liqueur into the sterilized presentation bottle(s) and store in a cool, dark place. To enjoy Nocino at its mellow, smooth best, you should ideally wait a year. But it is certainly very pleasant to drink after the 80-day wait.

The innocuous-looking juice from the walnuts will permanently stain anything it comes into contact with, including you. Gloves are highly recommended, and use a nonabsorbent board when chopping them—but the end result is completely worth it.

The ancient Celts can lay claim to this walnut liqueur. For them, it heralded the start of the summer, when it was made, and the end of summer, when it was drunk. The Italians are famous for making their version of it, Nocino, and mighty delicious it is too.

Sloe GIN

This is a traditional sweet liqueur and the measurements here work beautifully for a liqueur that you can sip on its own or in a cocktail such as Sloe Time (see page 156). The astringent, mouth-puckering, but beautiful blue-purple berries from the blackthorn will yield their magic infused in gin/vodka/whisky after 2 months, but the flavor after 6 months will be so much better, because you will gain some of the complex, aromatic bitterness from the pits (stones) inside the sloes.

1 pound (450g) sloes
1 cup (200g) superfine (caster) sugar
1 liter bottle of gin

1-quart (1-liter) wide-mouthed, sealable jar, sterilized (see page 33)
Sealable presentation bottle(s), sterilized (see page 33)

Makes approximately 1 quart (1 liter)

Wash and dry the sloes with a dishtowel. Put them in a freezer bag in a freezer overnight to simulate the frost effect. The skins will split as they thaw and save you the job of pricking each berry laboriously with a needle to help release the juices.

Place the frozen sloes in the sterilized jar and pour over the sugar, followed by the gin. Seal the jar and gently upend a couple of times, then store in a cool, dark place. After 3–6 months, strain the sloes into a wide-mouthed pitcher. Funnel into the sterilized presentation bottle(s).

ALTERNATIVE METHOD

You can omit the sugar at the start of the recipe and add sugar in the form of Simple Syrup (see page 68) to taste, at the end of the process, before bottling.

> **Many Sloe Gin recipes suggest that you upend the jar every other day but if you can wait 6 months, there is no need, as the sugar will gradually dissolve over the months, and the syrupy juices of the sloes will combine with the gin.**

SLOE VODKA

Simply replace the gin with vodka.

SLOE WHISKY

Use a blended Scotch whisky instead of gin, and replace the sugar with honey syrup, made with 1 cup (340g) runny honey and 1 cup (250ml) water. Let the syrup cool before adding it in exactly the same way as sugar.

EPINÉ

It is to France that we turn with gratitude for coming up with the idea of an apéritif made from the leaves of the humble blackthorn or sloe (*Prunus spinosa*). Simply by combining the blackthorn leaves with red wine and brandy or, as I did here, with apple eau de vie, you will have a beautiful, almond-like apéritif. It is delicious on its own and combines beautifully with fennel for an Epiné and Fennel Negroni (see page 183).

Foragers are besotted with sloe berries, using them for gin/vodka/whisky liqueurs—and, to a lesser extent, with sloe blossom flowers to make an almondy syrup—but it is this red-wine-based aperitif using the leaves that shows off the all-round versatility of this amazing hedgerow shrub.

2 large handfuls of blackthorn leaves
1 cup (250ml) apple eau de vie or brandy
1 quart (1 liter) red wine
1 cup (200g) superfine (caster) sugar

1-quart (1-liter) wide-mouthed, sealable jar, sterilized (see page 33)
Presentation bottle(s), sterilized (see page 33)

Makes approximately 1½ quarts (1.5 liters)

Place the blackthorn leaves in the sterilized jar. Pour in the eau de vie or brandy, making sure that the leaves are completely covered. Seal the jar and let the leaves infuse for 5 days to extract the maximum flavor.

Strain the infusion into a wide-mouthed pitcher. Then pour 1 cup (250ml) of the infusion back into the cleaned jar. Add the red wine and sugar. Seal the jar and upend it gently a couple of times. Leave for 2 weeks before funneling into the presentation bottle(s). Store in a cool, dark place for up to a year. This liqueur definitely improves with age, but it is important that the bottles are properly sealed.

Quince and Medlar LIQUEUR

Purists would probably not put these two ancient fruits together, but I didn't have enough of either to make the liqueur I wanted, so I did—and loved the result. The best quince to use is the European quince (*Cydonia oblonga*). The medlar, a relative of the apple, needs to be allowed to "blet," to get that wonderful, caramel-like pear and date flavor. The word comes from the French, *blettir*, which means "to soften by undergoing the initial stages of decomposition." To get the best mellow flavor, this liqueur benefits from a few months of patience.

3 medium quinces
18oz (500g) bletted medlars
2½ cups (500g) superfine (caster) sugar
1 liter bottle of vodka

½-gallon (2-liter) wide-mouthed sealable jar, sterilized (see page 33)
Sealable presentation bottle(s), sterilized (see page 33)

Makes approximately 1 quart (1 liter)

Wash and dry the quinces with a dishtowel. Chop into small pieces with a sharp knife, leaving on the skin but removing the core, and add to the sterilized jar. Pierce each bletted medlar with a knife several times and add to the jar. Cover the chopped fruit with sugar. Add the vodka. Seal and upend the jar gently a couple of times and store in a cool, dark place. Upend every day for the first week or so, until the sugar has dissolved. Leave for at least 6 months for the best mellow flavor.

Strain the liquid into a wide-mouthed pitcher—you may need to do this a couple of times or use a coffee filter or cheesecloth to get a clear liquid. Funnel into the presentation bottle(s) and seal. Store in a cool, dark place and consume within a year.

To blet medlars, pick them when still golden, if possible, and place on a tray, without them touching, in a cool place, like a garden shed. Leave them until they become soft to the touch (and brown), but not rotten. The taste is much nicer than the look!

Quinces, related to the pear, are incredibly sour when eaten raw but they turn sweet, with an almost pineapple fragrance, when sugar is added.

VARIATION

Use an inexpensive brandy instead of the vodka.

Lemon Balm LIQUEUR

The sweet, citrussy flavour of lemon balm (*Melissa officinalis*) makes this herb a great ingredient in many cocktails, such as the Lemon Balm and Nasturtium Daisy (see page 145). If you can get your hands on a cultivar of lemon balm called *M. officinalis* 'Quedlinburger Niederliegende', go for it, because it has a particularly high concentration of essential oils and therefore fragrance.

3 cups (100g) organic lemon balm leaves

Zest of 3 unwaxed, organic lemons (see page 15)

1 liter bottle of vodka, 80 proof/40% ABV

1 cup (200g) superfine (caster) sugar (optional)

1-quart (1-liter) wide-mouthed sealable jar, sterilized (see page 33)

Sealable presentation bottle(s), sterilized (see page 33)

Makes approximately 1 quart (1 liter)

Gently wash and dry the lemon balm leaves. Slap them between your hands to release the essential oil, then place in the sterilized jar. Add the lemon zest, vodka, and sugar. Seal the jar and upend it gently a couple of times. Store in a cool, dark place for a month, turning it every other day.

Strain the liquid into a wide-mouthed pitcher. Taste. If you would like a sweeter liqueur, make a simple syrup by heating equal parts of superfine (caster) sugar and water, let it cool, and add to the liqueur until you have the desired level of sweetness. Funnel into the sterilized presentation bottle(s). This is another liqueur that is great to store in the freezer. Use within a year.

> Lemon balm is said to be good for stress and anxiety. Pick it early in the morning after the dew has dried, when it will be at its most aromatic.

Wild Cherry PLUM BRANDY

Wild cherry plums (*Prunus cerasifera*) are completely different from wild cherries, though they look similar, and can be found in city streets and hedgerows across the Northern Hemisphere. The yellow or red fruits usually ripen in mid- or late summer, but most of them are left untouched by passers-by, unaware of the deliciousness that would ensue if they introduced them to some brandy. This liqueur works magnificently in a Wild Plum Smash (see page 156).

About 50 wild cherry plums

1½ cups (300g) superfine (caster) sugar

700 or 750ml bottle of brandy, 80 proof/40% ABV, mid-price range

1-quart (1-liter) wide-mouthed, sealable jar, sterilized (see page 33)

Sealable presentation bottle(s), sterilized (see page 33)

Makes approximately 1½ pints (750ml)

Wash and dry the wild cherry plums with a dishtowel, then score with a sharp knife, leaving the pits (stones) inside. Place them in the sterilized jar, add the sugar, and then top with the brandy. Seal the jar, upend it gently a couple of times, and store in a cool, dark place. Turn it every day until the sugar dissolves. After that, you can ignore it and leave for a total minimum of 3 months.

As the pits are still in the fruits, strain and funnel the liquid after 4 months at the most to prevent any mold forming. The liquid should then be completely clear, but to be on the safe side, strain it again into a wide-mouthed pitcher and then funnel into the presentation bottle(s). Consume within a year.

Wild cherry plums taste undoubtedly of plums, but if you want to be sure of their identity before biting into them, look for fruit hanging individually along the branch and for leaves that are small and finely toothed at the point.

Use a mid-range, high-proof brandy, rather than anything fancy, as you are going to be adding a very flavorsome fruit as well as sugar to it.

THE SWEET

Most cocktails need a sweetener to balance out the acidity and bitterness, but moderation is the key. Apart from being unhealthy for you, over-sweetened cocktails create a sickly mouth-feel and mask other flavors. When you are using fantastic base spirits and fresh or natural ingredients, there is far less need for sugar. Fresh fruits provide their own, and there are some plants that can be employed very effectively to create the desired level of sweetness.

Many recipes will call for simple syrup (1:1 sugar to water) or rich simple syrup (2:1 sugar to water) to give the cocktail the necessary sweetness. Both are made in the same way (see below).

Of course, it's healthy to move away from refined white sugar and, where possible, use raw cane and brown sugars. Agave nectar, honey, maple, and birch syrups are all great sugar alternatives and bring their own flavors and colors, but you need to understand their flavor profiles and the difference they will make to the color of a drink. I still use white superfine (caster) sugar when I want a brighter, clearer syrup. And I use granulated sugar for jams, jellies, and preserves too, which is another way of giving masses of flavor and a pleasing body to a cocktail sweetener (see Sloe Time, page 156).

SIMPLE SYRUP

Heat the sugar and water on a low heat and stir until the sugar is thoroughly dissolved. Add a tablespoon of 80 proof/40% ABV vodka to increase the syrup's shelf life. Once cooled, funnel into a sterilized bottle and store in the refrigerator for up to 2 weeks—up to a month if you have added vodka.

You can omit the heating process and simply combine equal amounts of sugar and water in a bottle or jar, then seal and shake vigorously until the sugar is dissolved, but the syrup won't be quite as thick.

Sugar ALTERNATIVES

The leaves of the South American plant *Stevia rebaudiana* are a natural sweetener—30–45 times sweeter than sugar. Some people claim that the leaves also help control levels of blood sugar, cholesterol, and blood pressure. We are trying to grow the plant for the first time in the garden at Midnight Apothecary, but it's not easy—overwintering is a particular problem.

Using fresh stevia leaves in cocktail recipes is not all plain sailing, though, as each plant can vary in the amount of sweetness it offers. There is also an undeniable aniseed, almost bitter, aftertaste, which depends on the amount of stevioside, the sweet element, contained in each plant. If the leaves are infused for too long in a syrup, or are used fresh in delicately flavored cocktails, the taste can be quite unpleasant. Although stevia leaves don't provide the same consistency that sugar gives to a syrup, you can use them to make a 3:1 (water to stevia) simple syrup (see below) for robustly flavored cocktails where there is already a strong texture created by fruit or dairy ingredients.

SWEET CICELY (*Myrrhis odorata*) not only looks beautiful in the garden but the leaves can also be used as a sweetener in anything with rhubarb or gooseberries (see Rhubarb and Ginger Syrup, page 79), which is what we do at Midnight Apothecary. You can halve the amount of sugar in a simple syrup recipe by adding chopped cicely leaves, but they do have an aniseed taste, so use cautiously.

AGAVE NECTAR, from the blue agave plant, is also sweeter than sugar. While it registers very low on the glycemic index, its very high fructose content is not good news. On the bright side, you can get away with using about a third less of it when a recipe calls for simple syrup. However, its golden or dark brown color will affect the look of the cocktail.

HONEY is a fantastic ingredient, both for the flavor of the flowers, on which the bees have been gorging, and for its health-giving properties. It is too thick to use on its own, so simply combine equal parts honey and water, and heat until the honey is thoroughly dissolved to give a delicious floral simple syrup.

Instead of adding sugar or syrup to a drink, you can put it on the rim of the glass or on a honey swizzle stick and turn it into a lollipop. This allows your guests to control the amount of sweetness they have in their mouth and when—and it also looks fun. They can suck on the lollipop or stir it into their drink while enjoying the bitterness of a great apéritif or digestif.

STEVIA SYRUP

Pour 1 cup (250ml) of warm water over 1 handful of stevia leaves. Let them steep for 12 hours, strain, and refrigerate. Use within a week. You can also try stevia alongside other strong-flavored natural sweeteners like honey and maple syrup to reduce their amounts in a recipe.

FLAVORED SYRUPS

Infusing a simple syrup with fresh ingredients gives a cocktail outstanding flavor and sweetness. As with all elements of cocktail mixology, you will find a host of methods claiming to be the best. The recipes on the following pages use a hot, or rapid, infusion technique for great results, achieved very quickly and easily. A cold infusion (maceration) or a sous vide method (using a vacuum-sealed bag in a water bath) to extract the flavors at a specific low temperature (around 140°F/60°C) can result in a brighter, clearer syrup of outstanding purity, but life may be just a little too short if you are doing this for fun.

The joy of making flavored syrups is that you can drink them on their own as a soda, with lots of ice and water, or incorporate them into a cocktail of your choice. In the recipes that follow, I have used sugar as the common ingredient for a syrup. If you have access to stevia or sweet cicely, please experiment by using them as described on page 69.

Ginger SYRUP

This syrup will come in handy, not just for your cocktails, such as the Nasturtium Collins (see page 144), but also for a variety of gastronomic delights like marinades, stir fries, and desserts.

2 cups (400g) superfine (caster) sugar

2 cups (500ml) water

2½oz (75g) fresh ginger, fairly thickly sliced

1 tbsp lemon juice or 80 proof/40% ABV vodka (optional)

Sealable presentation bottle(s), sterilized (see page 33)

Makes approximately 1 pint (500ml)

Place the sugar and water in a nonreactive pan and slowly bring to a boil. Add the ginger and let simmer for 5 minutes. Remove from the heat and let the ginger steep for another 10 minutes.

Strain the syrup into a wide-mouthed pitcher and then funnel into the sterilized presentation bottle(s) and seal. Store in the refrigerator and consume within 2 weeks. A tablespoon of lemon juice or high-proof vodka added just after removing the pan from the heat will increase the shelf life of the syrup for up to a month.

> Once you have made the syrup, sprinkle the ginger slices on top of vanilla ice cream to make a grown-up dessert, or dip them in granulated sugar, for candied ginger, which you can serve on its own as candy or as a pretty cocktail garnish.

WILD VIOLET *Syrup*

Although this very sweet and floral syrup is a fiddle to make because the wild violet (*Viola odorata*) flowers are tiny and you need a lot of them, and the petals also have to be removed individually from their stems and flower centers, I think it is really worth it. The color is extraordinary, and it is perfect for the Wild Violet Sour (see page 160).

7 large handfuls of wild violet petals, stems and flower centers removed

2 cups (500ml) boiling water

Approximately 2 cups (400g) granulated sugar

1 tbsp lemon juice (optional)

1 tbsp vodka (optional)

1-quart (1-liter) wide-mouthed, heatproof, and sealable jar, sterilized (see page 33)

Sealable presentation bottle(s), sterilized (see page 33)

Makes approximately 1 pint (500ml)

Place the petals in the jar, pour the boiling water over them, and seal. Let the petals infuse for 12 hours.

Strain the liquid into a measuring cup, then pour into a nonreactive pan. For every cup of liquid, add 1 cup (200g) of sugar. Heat gently until the sugar has dissolved—make sure it does not boil, as the blue color will take on a gray tinge. Once cooled, funnel into the sterilized presentation bottle(s) and seal. If you are not happy with the color, use a dropper or pipette to add lemon juice, drop by drop, until you reach the perfect shade of lavender/violet. (If desired, add a tablespoon of vodka to make the syrup last longer.) Seal and store in the refrigerator. Use within 3 months.

> Although the syrup starts off blue, it will change to a translucent lavender when mixed with water, then turn bright magenta when combined with an acid, such as lemon juice, or green if mixed with something alkaline. You decide which you prefer.

Honeysuckle SYRUP

A hedgerow or wall covered in wild honeysuckle (*Lonicera periclymenum*) is
a heady and erotic feast for the senses. *Lonicera japonica* is equally sweet and
delicious and, like wild honeysuckle, can be found naturalized across Europe
and North America, scrambling over gardens, walls, and wasteland. Honeysuckle
has the strongest scent at night, so try to harvest unopened and newly opened
flowers during the evening (how's that for a romantic date suggestion?) or early
morning. Use the syrup in a soda or The Honeysuckle (see page 180).

**8 large handfuls of unsprayed
honeysuckle flowers, leaves and
stems removed**

**Approximately 2 cups (400g)
superfine (caster) sugar**

Juice of ½ lemon

**Sealable presentation bottle(s),
sterilized (see page 33)**

Makes approximately 1 pint (500ml)

Place the honeysuckle flowers in
a nonreactive bowl and cover with
cold water, then leave to steep for
12 hours, or at least overnight, at
room temperature. Make sure the
flowers are completely covered by
the water.

Strain the mixture into a measuring
cup, discarding the flowers. Pour
the liquid into a nonreactive pan.
Measure an equal amount of sugar
to the liquid and add to the pan.
Bring to a boil, and let simmer for
5 minutes. Feel free to replace half
the sugar with a handful of chopped
sweet cicely leaves, but bear in mind
that this will adjust the color.

Remove from the heat, let cool, add
the lemon juice, and funnel into the
sterilized presentation bottle(s).

There is some debate about the toxicity of certain species of honeysuckle, their berries in particular, so stick to *Lonicera periclymenum* and *L. japonica*, and leave the berries alone.

★

The name "honeysuckle" comes from the traditional practice of sucking the tiny drop of honey-flavored nectar from the flowers.

Rose Petal SYRUP

This recipe involves massage, roses, and perfume... don't blame me if things get out of hand! I would recommend using the most perfumed roses you can find, and definitely make sure they are unsprayed. It also helps if their petals are quite thin. Two good choices that grow wild and adorn many a private and public space are *Rosa rugosa* and the wild dog rose, *R. canina*. Whenever I use wild dog rose, which has very delicate pink petals, I add a few petals of a red rose to give a really rich-colored syrup.

6 handfuls of pink and/or red rose petals

6 cups (1.2kg) superfine (caster) sugar

3 cups (750ml) water

Zest of ½ unwaxed, organic orange (see page 15)

1 tbsp lemon juice

Pinch of salt

Sealable presentation bottle(s), sterilized (see page 33)

Makes approximately 1½ pints (750ml)

Snip off the bitter white tip at the base of each petal—it's a little awkward to do but worth it. Alternatively, when picking the petals from the rosebush, pull the petals in a clump with one hand and snip the base off in one go with the other.

Loosely pack the petals in a nonreactive bowl and add about 2 cups (400g) of the sugar. Gently massage the sugar into the petals to bruise them and start the maceration. Cover with a clean dishtowel and leave overnight or up to 12 hours.

You should return to a gooey mess, where the petals have shrunk and the sugar has extracted some color and flavor out of them. Tip this sugar and petal mix into a nonreactive pan, add the remaining sugar, water, orange zest, lemon juice, and a pinch of salt, and gently bring to a boil. You will notice that the color transfers from the petals into the liquid. Let simmer for 5 minutes or until you have a thick, unctuous syrup.

Let the syrup cool. Strain it into a wide-mouthed pitcher, then funnel into the sterilized presentation

These roses need plenty of sunshine to maximize their fragrance and, ideally, you should pick newly open petals in the morning, after the dew has dried but before the heat of the sun takes its toll.

Try to pick only the petals, as that will allow the hips to grow, which you can harvest later in the year for rosehip jelly or syrup.

bottle(s) and seal. You can store the syrup in the refrigerator for well over a month. As this is a rich simple syrup, you need only very small quantities in your sodas and cocktails.

Gorse Flower SYRUP

You will find carpets of gorse (*Ulex europaeus*) by the coast, on heathland, in town parks, and on wasteland. The pain of harvesting the beautiful acid-yellow flowers from this extremely dense, spiny shrub is worth it for the coconut and almond-tasting syrup. Eat them raw to savor that flavor.

4 large handfuls of gorse flowers

2 cups (400g) superfine (caster) sugar

4 cups (1 liter) water

Juice of ½ lemon

Zest of ½ unwaxed, organic orange (see page 15), without any white pith

Sealable presentation bottle(s), sterilized (see page 33)

Makes approximately 1 quart (1 liter)

De-bug the gorse flowers and remove any greenery or spines. Combine the sugar and water in a pan until the solution reaches boiling point. Take off the heat and immediately add the unwashed flowers, lemon juice, and orange zest. Let cool.

Strain the liquid into a wide-mouthed pitcher, then funnel into the sterilized presentation bottle(s) and seal immediately. The syrup will keep for 1 month in the refrigerator but it won't if you make some Gorse Collins (see page 161)!

> **Gorse flowers are very high in protein, so, if you find yourself lost and alone in the wilderness, this plant could really help you out.**

Charred Sage SYRUP

There are several ways to smoke a liquid. You can use a hand-held culinary smoker to instantly infuse a syrup or spirit while making your cocktail. However, the method here is old-school, fun to do, and produces a depth of earthy, campfire smokiness that evokes woodland, and the aroma lasts as long as the syrup— perfect for a Woodland Martini (see page 170). I've used a dark honey here but agave nectar would also produce an earthy, dark syrup.

1 cup (340g) dark wildflower honey
1 cup (250ml) water
10 large sage leaves on a stem

Sealable presentation bottle, sterilized (see page 33)

Makes approximately ½ pint (250ml)

Combine the honey and water in a nonreactive pan over a medium heat and stir to help the honey dissolve into the sugar. Meanwhile, hold the sage leaves by the end of their stalks and singe their tips with a long lighter until you see red cinders, the odd flame, and charred leaves.

Snip off the bitter stalks of the sage and drop the charred leaves into the pan with the honey syrup. Bring the syrup to a boil, then simmer for about 8 minutes. Turn off the heat and let cool.

Pour the liquid through a strainer lined with layers of cheesecloth or muslin into a wide-mouthed pitcher, then funnel into the sterilized presentation bottle and seal. Store in the refrigerator and consume within 3 months.

If you make this syrup around the campfire, be sure to use a really fine-mesh strainer, or several layers of cheesecloth or muslin, or a coffee filter, because the tiny specks of ash from the charred sage don't look attractive or taste nice.

Rhubarb and Ginger SYRUP

This is a fantastic-looking as well as tasting syrup, especially if you find really red rhubarb stalks. At Midnight Apothecary, we use the leftover "jam" in a Sloe Time (see page 156), and the syrup in a Rhubarbra Collins (see page 131). Sweet cicely grows and works perfectly with rhubarb as a natural sweetener. If you don't have any, just omit and double the amount of sugar.

4 cups (700g) bright red rhubarb, cut into 1-in (2.5-cm) slices
1½oz (40g) fresh ginger, grated
1 cup (200g) superfine (caster) sugar
4 tbsp (10g) finely chopped sweet cicely (*Myrrhis odorata*) leaves
2 cups (500ml) water
1–2 thin slices of fresh ginger (optional)
1 tbsp vodka (optional)

Sealable presentation bottle(s), sterilized (see page 33)

Makes approximately 1½ pints (750ml)

Place all the main ingredients in a nonreactive pan and bring to a boil over a medium heat. Let simmer until the rhubarb disintegrates and becomes pulpy (usually about 15–20 minutes). While the liquid is still piping hot, strain into a wide-mouthed pitcher and then funnel into the sterilized presentation bottle(s) and seal. Add a slice or two of ginger if you want to accentuate the ginger notes.

Store in the refrigerator and consume within 2 weeks. Add a tablespoon of vodka to make it last longer.

This syrup is good value, as you can use the rhubarb and ginger leftovers as a compote on yogurt or ice cream.

CHOCOLATE MINT *Syrup*

The menthol in peppermint often makes it too sharp for cocktails, but there is an exception: chocolate mint (*Mentha × piperata* f. *citrata* 'Chocolate'). I am combining it with spearmint (*M. spicata*), also known as garden, or common, mint, in this recipe, as I want the gorgeous chocolate undertones of after-dinner mints but not too much peppermint. If you don't have chocolate mint, just double up on whichever mint you do have. Use in a Chocolate Mint Julep (see page 115).

1 cup (250ml) water

1 cup (200g) superfine (caster) sugar

½ cup (about 15) unsprayed chocolate mint leaves, stalks removed

½ cup (about 15) unsprayed spearmint leaves, stalks removed

Sealable, heatproof presentation bottle, sterilized (see page 33)

Makes approximately ½ pint (250ml)

Stir the water and sugar together in a nonreactive pan over a low heat and let simmer for 2 minutes. Smack the unwashed mint leaves between your palms to release the oils and drop them into the pan. Immediately remove the pan from the heat. Let the leaves infuse for 10 minutes—no longer or you will lose some of the freshness of the mint and it will start to take on bitterness.

While still piping hot, strain the liquid into a wide-mouthed pitcher, then funnel into the sterilized presentation bottle and seal. Store in the refrigerator for up to 2 weeks.

Many flavored mint cultivars—lime, pineapple, eau de cologne, and berries and cream—smell delicious when you rub the leaves, but they often taste quite vegetal. For that reason, I tend to stick to spearmint (*Mentha spicata*), also known as garden, or common, mint, and spearmint cultivars such as *M. spicata* var. *crispa* 'Moroccan'.

THYME SYRUP

Replace the mint with the leaves from 4 sprigs of thyme (*Thymus vulgaris*), wild thyme (*T. serpyllum*), or lemon thyme (*T. citriodorus*), each about the length of a finger.

ROSEMARY SYRUP

Replace the mint with the needles from 3 small sprigs of rosemary (*Rosmarinus officinalis*), each about the length of a finger.

Lemon Verbena and Raspberry SYRUP

Lemon verbena (*Aloysia citrodora*) is just about my favorite herb. It's nothing to look at—although the tiny, lavender-white flowers on this tall, leggy shrub are quite cute—but the smell and taste of those little leaves pack such a lemony, aromatic, sweet punch. You really don't need many of them to get fantastic results. It's a natural bedfellow for raspberries, and this syrup forms the sweet component in the Raspberry and Scented Geranium Sour (see pages 140–41).

2 cups (500ml) water

2 cups (400g) superfine (caster) sugar (you could substitute half the sugar with 2 tbsp/5g or 2 young stems of sweet cicely (*Myrrhis odorata*) leaves, finely chopped, for a slight aniseed flavor)

1 cup (125g) raspberries

4 lemon verbena leaves

Sealable, heatproof presentation bottle(s), sterilized (see page 33)

Makes approximately 1 pint (500ml)

Stir the water and sugar together in a nonreactive pan over a low heat to make a simple syrup. Once it has reached boiling point, add the raspberries and lemon verbena leaves, stir, and let simmer until the raspberries have collapsed (about 10 minutes).

Strain while still piping hot, but not boiling, into a wide-mouthed pitcher—you really don't want raspberry pips in this syrup—then funnel into the sterilized presentation bottle(s). Seal and store in the refrigerator for up to 2 weeks. The remaining raspberry (with the lemon verbena solids removed) can be used as a compote over yogurt or ice cream.

RASPBERRY AND THYME SYRUP

For this syrup, used in the Clover Club (see page 119), replace the lemon verbena with a handful of fresh thyme leaves (about 10 sprigs), stripped from the stalks.

Lemon verbena is not fully hardy and likes very free-draining, sandy, poor soil. If you don't have the right growing conditions, keep it in a pot in a frost-free place over winter and plant out once the soil warms up.

Lilac SYRUP

The humble fragrant lilac (*Syringa vulgaris*) makes a delightful syrup for use in a soda or a Blackberry and Lilac Cobbler (see page 178). If its color turns out a bit insipid, add a couple of mahonia berries, blackberries, or blueberries to darken it.

2 cups (about 6 heads) lilac blossoms

1 cup (200g) superfine (caster) sugar

1 cup (250ml) water

Zest of ½ unwaxed, organic orange (see page 15)

1 tbsp lemon juice

Sealable presentation bottle, sterilized (see page 33)

Makes approximately ½ pint (250ml)

De-bug the blossoms and remove them from the green bitter stems.

Place the sugar and water in a nonreactive pan and stir over a low heat until it boils. Add the unwashed lilac blossoms and orange zest, and bring back to a boil. Simmer for 10 minutes. Add the lemon juice. Strain the liquid into a wide-mouthed pitcher while still piping hot, then funnel into the sterilized presentation bottle and seal. Store in a refrigerator and use within 1 month.

There are two species of mahonia you are likely to come across: *Mahonia japonica* and *M. aquifolium* (the Oregon grape), which has much rounder fruit. The berries of both are great for making syrups but those of the latter make an attractive garnish too.

★

Be warned: as you pick the berries, your hands, and everything you touch, will start to run with a blood-colored juice, resembling some kind of massacre.

Mahonia SYRUP

Mahonias are as tough as old boots and provide year-round interest with their racemes of yellow flowers, followed by amazing purple berries, which resemble grapes. Instead of picking berries from shrubs in public spaces, which could have been sprayed with pesticides or be full of carbon monoxide, I prefer to ask people if I can pick a few from their yard. This syrup is superb in an Only the Mahonia (see page 200).

4 cups (500g) ripe mahonia (*M. japonica* or *M. aquifolium*) berries

2 cups (500ml) water

2 cups (400g) superfine (caster) sugar

Sealable, heatproof presentation bottle(s), sterilized (see page 33)

Makes approximately 1 pint (500ml)

Remove the berries from their stems—when ripe, they will come off very easily. Check for bugs and give the berries a rinse.

Place the berries in a nonreactive pan with the water and heat slowly. You will notice the color of the water changing almost immediately to a dark purple. As soon as the water starts to bubble, remove the pan from the heat, gently mash the berries to release any more juice, and strain into a wide-mouthed measuring cup.

Pour into a clean nonreactive pan. For each cup (250ml) of liquid, measure out the same amount of sugar and add to the pan. Bring to a boil over a medium heat, then simmer for 5 minutes. While the liquid is still piping hot, funnel into the sterilized presentation bottle(s), seal, and store in the refrigerator for up to 2 weeks.

Meadowsweet SYRUP

Clouds of creamy, fluffy meadowsweet (*Filipendula ulmaria*) blossom appear on Walthamstow Marshes in east London, not far from Midnight Apothecary, during early and mid-summer. Interspersed with pink and purple wild vetches and peas, they are a beautiful sight, and the heady, almond, vanilla, and honey scent is easily transferred to an exquisite syrup, which I actually prefer to elderflower cordial. One of our most popular cocktails in the summer that uses this syrup is The Mighty Meadowsweet (see page 154).

15 heads of meadowsweet blossoms, fully opened

4 cups (1 liter) water

5 cups (1kg) superfine (caster) sugar

Zest and juice of 1 unwaxed, organic lemon (see page 15)

Sealable presentation bottle(s), sterilized (see page 33)

Makes approximately 1 quart (1 liter)

Strip the meadowsweet blossoms from the stems and stalks, and put to one side to give the wildlife plenty of time to evacuate.

Make a simple syrup by heating the sugar and water in a nonreactive pan over a low heat, stirring to dissolve the sugar. Once it reaches boiling point, remove the pan from the heat. Add the lemon zest and flowers. Submerge the flowers in the syrup, cover, and leave overnight or up to 12 hours, to infuse.

Add the lemon juice, stir, then strain into a wide-mouthed pitcher to remove the flowers and lemon zest. Reheat the syrup gently in a clean nonreactive pan and funnel into the sterilized presentation bottle(s) while still piping hot. Seal the bottle.

Store somewhere cool and dark. Once opened, keep in the refrigerator for 2 to 3 months.

> The name meadowsweet comes from the plant's traditional job of flavoring and sweetening mead. In medieval times, stems of meadowsweet were also used to sweeten the air.
>
>
>
> The leaves and stalks taste vegetal and medicinal when boiled, so make sure you strip the flowers from their stalks with your fingers (very easily done) or a fork before adding them to the pan.

Elderberry and Clove SYRUP

As well as having a rich, earthy fruitiness, this syrup, made from the most common of shrubs, *Sambucus nigra*, is best known as a winter tonic, boosting the immune system and helping to fight flu, either as a preventive medicine or as a symptomatic treatment. This recipe is used as a base for Elderberry Me (see page 169), where I can only hope the goodness of the elderberries in some way mitigates any harm done by the consumption of heavy (double) cream!

25 heads of elderberries
At least 4 cups (1 liter) water
3¾ cups (750g) superfine (caster) sugar
12 cloves

Sealable presentation bottle(s), sterilized (see page 33)

Makes approximately 1 quart (1 liter)

Elderberry stems and stalks are poisonous, and even the berries are slightly toxic if eaten raw in quantity, so make sure you strip the berries from the stalks and don't be tempted to munch on them.

Strip the berries from the stems using your fingers or a fork. Rinse the berries, then add to a nonreactive pan. Pour in enough water to cover them (at least 1 quart/1 liter). Bring to a boil and let simmer on a low heat until the berries are softened (about 20 minutes).

Mash the berries gently to ensure all the juice has been released. Remove from the heat and strain the berries into a wide-mouthed measuring cup. You should have just over 1 quart (1 liter) of juice. Add the sugar and cloves. Return the liquid, sugar, and cloves to the cleaned pan and bring to a boil. Let simmer for a further 10 minutes. Remove from the heat and funnel into the sterilized presentation bottle(s). Divide the cloves up equally between the bottles and seal.

Store in a cool, dark place, where the syrup will last for up to a year. Once opened, keep in the refrigerator for up to 2 months. You may wish to remove the cloves after a time if their flavor becomes too strong.

Rosehip SYRUP

At Midnight Apothecary, we use hedgerow syrups like this in colorful autumnal cocktails, such as Berried Treasure (see page 172), where jewels of concentrated fruit flavor burst in your mouth in an otherwise grown-up cocktail. They also work very well in Sours, where lemon juice and egg white balance the sweetness. The huge hips of the Japanese rose (*Rosa rugosa*) are excellent for this completely delicious syrup, as their large size means less chopping.

2¼ pounds (1kg) rosehips
About 3 quarts (3 liters) water
5 cups (1kg) superfine (caster) sugar
Juice of ½ lemon or 1 tbsp vodka

Sealable presentation bottle(s), sterilized (see page 33)

Makes approximately 1 quart (1 liter)

Wash and chop the rosehips in half. Bring 1½ quarts (1.5 liters) of the water to a boil in a large, nonreactive pan. Add the rosehips. Return to a boil, simmer for 5 minutes, and remove from the heat. Let cool slightly.

Strain the rosehip mixture carefully through a jelly bag or layers of cheesecloth suspended above a large bowl. Put the pulp back in the cleaned pan with the remaining 1½ quarts (1.5 liters) of water, bring to a boil, remove from the heat, and strain again as above.

Combine the juice from both strains with the sugar and bring to a boil. Boil hard for at least 10 minutes or until you get a thick, syrupy consistency. Remove from the heat and add the lemon juice or tablespoon of vodka. Funnel into the sterilized presentation bottle(s).

Rosehips provide another one of those incredibly common, colorful, and health-preserving syrups that are jam-packed with vitamin C and other goodies to keep us healthy through the winter months.

This recipe repeats the straining process to produce as much syrup as possible. I also use several layers of cheesecloth to make sure that the tiny irritants inside the rosehip are removed.

Crab Apple SYRUP

This beautiful, orangey-pink, floral-scented, autumnal syrup could not be further removed from the jaw-clenching sourness of a green or red uncooked crab apple. The recipe requires patience: the crab apple juice has to drip, drop by drop, through a very fine strainer or several layers of cheesecloth, otherwise it will turn cloudy. It's best to leave it overnight to resist the temptation of giving it a prod. It is delicious in a Hedgerow Sour (see page 157).

Red-skinned crab apples give the best color but even the green ones turn the most beautiful blush orange.

3¼ pounds (1.5kg) crab apples
3½ cups (700g) superfine (caster) sugar
Juice of ½ lemon

Sealable presentation bottle(s), sterilized (see page 33)

Makes approximately 1 quart (1 liter)

Wash the crab apples and remove any stems, greenery, and blossom ends. Don't bother to core the apples but if they are golf-ball size or bigger, cut them in half. Place in a nonreactive pan and pour in just enough water to cover. Bring to a boil and let simmer until the apples are soft (about 25 minutes).

Strain the pulp carefully through a jelly bag or several layers of cheesecloth suspended above a large bowl or pan. Let the pulp move through the filter very slowly.

Measure your final amount of juice, and for every 1 quart (1 liter), add 3½ cups (700g) sugar. Add the juice and sugar to the cleaned pan and bring to a boil. Then add the lemon juice and boil hard for about 10 minutes until you have a syrup consistency—you do not want a jelly, as that will be difficult to incorporate into cocktails. Skim off any froth.

Carefully funnel the syrup into the sterilized presentation bottle(s) and seal. Store in a cool, dark place. Once opened, consume within a month.

Rowan SYRUP

The berries from the rowan tree or mountain ash (*Sorbus aucuparia, S. americana,* or *S. sambucifolia*), which grows happily in cities and rural areas alike, are a wonderful prize. The syrup made from them provides a fruity sourness and a slight bitterness, and it is the most beautiful red color. It works really well with brandy or even as a replacement for it. At Midnight Apothecary, we use it to make the Rowan, Honey, and Lemon Foam for The Honeysuckle (see page 180), where it balances the sweetness and acidity of the honey and lemon. I include a tiny amount of salt to counteract some of the rowan's natural bitterness, but it is not absolutely necessary.

2¼ pounds (1kg) very ripe, bright red rowan berries

Approximately 2 quarts (2 liters) water

1 heaped tsp salt

3½ cups (700g) superfine (caster) sugar

Sealable presentation bottle(s), sterilized (see page 33)

Makes approximately 1 quart (1 liter)

Separate the rowan berries from their stalks, then wash and rinse the berries. Add to a nonreactive pan and pour in about 1 quart (1 liter) of water and the salt, making sure the berries are covered. Bring to a boil and simmer long enough for them to become soft (about 25 minutes). Remove from the heat.

Using a large jelly bag or several layers of cheesecloth or muslin, slowly strain the berries and liquid into a wide-mouthed pitcher. Return the pulp to the pan and add the remaining 1 liter of water. Bring to a boil, then remove from the heat. Strain the pulp, as above, into the pitcher. Return all the strained liquid to the cleaned pan, add the sugar, bring to a boil, and boil hard for 5 minutes. Remove from the heat.

Funnel the syrup into the presentation bottle(s) while still piping hot. Seal. Store in a cool, dark place. Once opened, keep in the refrigerator and use within a month.

Sloe Blossom SYRUP

This syrup has a subtle almond flavor. I suggest you make only 1 pint (500ml), partly because picking the blossoms of the sloe (*Prunus spinosa*), also known as the blackthorn, is quite difficult—they are set in among thorns very close to the stems—and also because the poor bees in early spring need all the pollen they can get. You also want there to be berries for harvesting later in the year and making into Sloe Gin (see page 62).

6 handfuls of blackthorn flowers
3 cups (750ml) water
2½ cups (500g) superfine (caster) sugar

Sealable presentation bottle(s), sterilized (see page 33)

Makes approximately 1 pint (500ml)

Place the sloe blossoms in a nonreactive pan of cold water, making sure the blossoms are covered, and leave for a few hours.

Slowly heat the water and blossoms until just below boiling point. Keep at this temperature for about 20 minutes.

Strain the blossoms into a wide-mouthed pitcher and return the liquid back to the cleaned pan. Add the sugar and bring to a boil. Let simmer for 5 minutes. Remove from the heat and funnel into the sterilized presentation bottle(s). Seal and store in a cool, dark place. Once opened, keep in the refrigerator and use within a month.

Try to pick the blossoms early in the morning on a dry day when they are laden with pollen—they should be as heady as possible.

Yarrow SYRUP

The flowers of yarrow (*Achillea millefolium*) are bitter and astringent, but when sweetened, they make a beautiful syrup. Delicate, with an almost lavender taste, the syrup works very well with tequila to make The Yarrow (see page 176). Tequila comes from the agave plant, so the nectar from the blue agave is the natural sweetener for this syrup.

2 tbsp yarrow flowers
2 cups (500ml) boiling water
1¼ cups (425g) agave nectar (or honey)
1½ cups (355ml) water

Sealable presentation bottle, sterilized (see page 33)

Makes approximately ¾ pint (375ml)

Remove any unwanted wildlife and stalks from the flower heads and place in a nonreactive pan. Pour the boiling water over the flowers and steep for 15 minutes. Strain the liquid into a wide-mouthed pitcher. Return this "tea" to the cleaned pan and add the agave nectar (or honey) and 1½ cups (355ml) water. Bring to a boil and let simmer for a couple of minutes. Remove from the heat for 15 minutes before funneling into the sterilized presentation bottle. Store in the refrigerator and consume within a couple of months.

SUGAR VARIATION

If you don't have agave nectar or honey, use 2 cups (400g) superfine (caster) sugar and 2 cups (500ml) water instead.

At Midnight Apothecary, we use the newly opened flowers of the white native yarrow, which blooms all over parks and wasteland any time from early summer, rather than other, more cultivated varieties bred for color and scent.

Yarrow (and tansy) contain trace amounts of thujone, which is a uterine stimulant, so should be avoided during pregnancy.

Tansy SYRUP

The brilliant yellow flowers of tansy (*Tanacetum vulgare*) appear in the summer near rivers, landslides, and roads—in fact, any grassy or bushy areas. The leaves of this herbaceous perennial have a strong, pungent aroma—you can smell the camphor—and a bitter, aromatic taste. As with yarrow (opposite), we make a "tea" but with the leaves instead of the flowers. We use the syrup in mocktails, such as Tansy Ever After (see page 194).

1 heaped tbsp tansy leaves
2 cups (500ml) boiling water
2 cups (400g) superfine (caster) sugar

Sealable presentation bottle(s), sterilized (see page 33)

Makes approximately 1 pint (500ml)

Roughly chop or tear the unwashed tansy leaves into small pieces and place in a nonreactive pan. Pour the boiling water over the leaves. Allow the tansy "tea" to steep for 15 minutes. Strain the liquid into a wide-mouthed pitcher. Return the liquid to the cleaned pan, add the sugar, and bring to a boil. Simmer for 2 minutes before removing from the heat. After 15 minutes, funnel the liquid into the sterilized presentation bottle(s). Store in the refrigerator and consume within a couple of months.

Tansy has been used for centuries as a remedy for arthritis and headaches, and in the 1980s, it was popular as a herbal remedy for migraines. Like yarrow, it contains trace amounts of thujone, so should be avoided during pregnancy, and used sparingly by everyone else.

THE BITTER TRUTH

Bitterness is a vital component of a good cocktail, balancing out the alcohol, sugar, and acidity. From an evolutionary standpoint, we are very sensitive to bitterness, as it alerts us to the potential presence of plant toxins by causing a dry, numbing sensation. However, it serves no direct nutritional purpose, although it has been used for centuries for its ability to trigger enzymes that stimulate the appetite and aid digestion.

The apéritifs that we drink today, such as vermouth, are based on medicinal wines made of bitter herbs with the addition of strong aromatic herbs. Digestifs, such as Amari, are liqueurs flavored with bitter herbs to aid digestion. Tinctures, which use distilled, high-proof spirits to carry and preserve the properties of the medicinal, aromatic herbs, often include bittering agents such as roots, bark, and peel. Bitters in cocktails are essentially tiny dashes of those tinctures.

We help the medicine go down either by putting the bitter herbs in sweet syrups or by disguising them in a variety of sweet/strong elements, to make the overall drink palatable. A third way is to add the merest concentrated dash from our bitters bottle.

You can think of bitters as the salt and pepper of a cocktail but when you look at the variety of ingredients used in bitters these days, you can think of it as the whole spice rack!

Luckily for foragers and gardeners (and anyone with access to the Internet), the source of several main bittering agents is close at hand. Rhubarb, artichoke leaves, burdock roots, angelica roots, wild cherry bark, gentian root, quassia bark (from South America), horehound, and wormwood (*Artemisia*) are readily available, though I would recommend sourcing your ingredients from reputable suppliers unless you are absolutely sure you know what you are doing.

BITTERS

While they may look like the work of witchcraft and hocus-pocus, there is no great mystery to bitters. They are essentially bitter and aromatic herbs and spices, tinctured in high-proof spirits.

Standard bitters will use roots, bark, and/or leaves as the bittering agent, with aromatic herbs and spices providing flavor and any medicinal properties. The list of bittering agents should make up no more than half of the ingredients, which means there is plenty of scope to add flavor with fruits, herbs, spices, flowers, and nuts. It is really important to use a high-proof alcohol to extract the flavors and properties from each ingredient and also to preserve the shelf life of the bitters. For those reasons, choose one that is at least 100 proof or 50% ABV (alcohol by volume).

Depending on your cocktail requirements, you may want to add a little sweetener to your bitters, in which case, consider honey, sugar, or plants like *Stevia rebaudiana* and sweet cicely (*Myrrhis odorata*). While there are a few off-the-shelf recipes for bitters that enable you to combine all your botanical ingredients in one taste-tested infusion, in reality it is far better to carry out the laborious task of infusing each ingredient separately, because they will all be ready at different times. When it comes to blending your

ingredients into the final bitters, you need to be able to adjust each element. In terms of how to taste each separate infusion to see if it is ready, try a couple of drops diluted in water. If you get a strong sense of the flavor, it is. If you don't, it isn't.

The Wild Cherry Bitters recipe (see pages 102–103) is a halfway house between tincturing each ingredient in alcohol and then waiting for different lengths of time to start combining them into your bitters. It saves a bit of time by grouping together the bittering and spice ingredients that take the same amount of time to infuse.

Wild VERMOUTH

There are two common types of vermouth—dry and sweet—although cocktail mixologists will waste no time in offering endless examples of sweet white, amber, rosé, and plenty of others in between. The essential components are a light white or rosé wine with bitter botanicals (bark, roots, leaves, herbs, spices, and flowers), simple syrup or caramel (if you are making a sweet vermouth), and a high-alcohol-content spirit to fortify it and help extract the botanicals. As well as providing bitterness, the botanicals have aromatic and floral qualities. The key to success is keeping them separate so that you can adjust the quantity of each one as you go, to find the right balance for you.

20 small, sealable glass jars (as used for jellies and jams), sterilized (see page 33)
Pipette
Digital scales
Sealable presentation bottle(s), sterilized (see page 33)

Makes a minimum of 1⅓ pints (650ml), but with 2 bottles of wine, this quantity can be doubled

> Cocktail classics such as the Martini, Negroni, and Manhattan all use vermouth as an essential but quiet component.

12ml mugwort (*Artemisia vulgaris*)
12ml false acacia blossoms
5ml cinnamon sticks
2ml dried gentian root
15ml orange peel
10ml bay leaves
12ml juniper berries
9ml coriander seeds
5ml meadowsweet flowers
8ml black peppercorns
5ml vanilla beans (pods)
15ml gorse flowers
5ml dried chamomile flowers
7ml yarrow leaf
10ml sage
5ml thyme
5ml wild fennel seeds
3ml Douglas fir needles
5ml star anise
800ml grappa, 100 proof/ 50% ABV (I used Marolo Grappa di Arneis Renesio)
700 or 750ml bottle of dry white wine, such as Pinot Grigio or Trebbiano
2 tbsp (25g) superfine (caster) sugar

There are two methods of infusing the ingredients: cold maceration over several days versus rapid, heat-based infusion for almost instant results (see page 42). I've had greater success making a rounded, smooth infusion using the cold method. Agreed, it's involved and long-winded—but, oh, so worth it! Digital scales, able to measure the tiniest amounts, down to 0.1mg, are essential. Accordingly, the amounts given in this recipe are all metric.

Please note that the weights of the botanicals listed here refer to the final liquid amount of each ingredient once it has been macerated. In practice, you should source about 20g of each of the dried/fresh ingredients below in order to have these quantities available to work with.

To macerate the botanicals, weigh a small quantity, about 20g, of each one and place separately in a sterilized glass jar. Cover each one with about twice the amount of grappa. You do not have to be exact— you simply need a maximum of about

20ml of liquid in each jar to play with at the end of the maceration.

Seal the jars and leave somewhere dark for a minimum of 5 days and for a maximum of 2 weeks, during which time each of the macerating botanicals will work their magic. You will know they are ready when you taste them and get a strong flavor. Separate the solids by straining each spirit in turn into a wide-mouthed pitcher. Then funnel back into their cleaned jars.

Heat about 550ml of the white wine and the sugar in a nonreactive pan over a low heat until the sugar is dissolved—the sugar will balance the bitterness of the botanicals and highlight all their different flavors. Bring the wine and sugar to a boil, then simmer gently for 2 minutes before cooling completely. Make sure that you have exactly 500ml of wine to use.

Now for the fun part. For every 500ml of wine, you need 150g of macerated botanicals (roughly 3:1 wine to botanicals), made up of tiny amounts of your separate "teas." Using the pipette and digital scales, so that you can work in minute quantities, start adding your botanicals to the wine (keeping notes as you go about exactly what you've added and in what quantity). Remember that some of the botanicals will be far stronger than others. If you take my recipe as a guide, you will see the sort of ratios that work for me. For example, I used 12ml of mugwort as the key bittering agent, but I balanced it with some more floral and sweeter ingredients, such as 12ml acacia blossoms, 5ml meadowsweet flowers, and 5ml vanilla beans, as well as using plenty of aromatics like wild fennel and coriander seeds. Taste the spirit after

each additional ingredient and tweak the quantities, as desired.

Once you have balanced the bitter/aromatic/floral tastes to your liking, you are pretty much there. Funnel your creation into the sterilized presentation bottle(s), seal, and refrigerate. I prefer to wait a day to allow all the ingredients to sit together. Remember, this is an aromatized wine, so it starts deteriorating the moment the seal is broken. Use within 2 months. If you intend to use it only in small quantities, consider bottling in smaller presentation bottles to lengthen the shelf life.

While edible blossoms are the visual feast on the top of a cocktail, vermouth provides the opportunity to show off the alchemy of using bitter, ugly, and overlooked botanicals growing in and under your garden to create something of beauty within the substance of the drink.

Beech Leaf NOYAU

This is a traditional British foraging recipe, made to be enjoyed in the spring, much as sloe gin was to be drunk in the fall. It, in turn, is based on a French noyau—a brandy flavored with almonds and the bitter pits of apricots. To qualify as a noyau, it must contain a spirit flavored with a bittering agent. This could be bark or nuts but in the British version, it is young beech (*Fagus sylvatica*) leaves. The recipe works equally well with the same amount of young blackcurrant leaves. Both provide delicate, herbal notes with the gin and brandy, which makes it a versatile cocktail ingredient.

3 large handfuls of very young beech leaves

700 or 750ml bottle of gin

1 cup (200g) superfine (caster) sugar or ⅔ cup (150ml) agave syrup or ¾ cup (150g) natural cane sugar

1 cup (250ml) water

¾ cup (200ml) brandy

1-quart (1-liter) wide-mouthed, sealable jar, sterilized (see page 33)

Sealable presentation bottle(s), sterilized (see page 33)

Makes approximately 1 quart (1 liter)

Remove any wildlife from the leaves and wash. Loosely fill the sterilized jar with the leaves until it is about half full. Add the gin, making sure that the leaves are fully immersed, so that they do not oxidize. Seal the jar and store in a cool, dark place for about 3 weeks. Strain the gin into a wide-mouthed pitcher to remove the leaves.

Add the sugar and water to a nonreactive pan and slowly bring to a boil to make a simple syrup. As soon as it reaches boiling point, remove from the heat and let cool before adding to the pitcher of gin. Add the brandy, stir, then funnel into the presentation bottle(s). Seal and upend gently a couple of times. Store in a cool, dark place and wait a minimum of 2 weeks to allow the flavors to combine—it improves with age.

This noyau is delicious on its own over ice or you can add a measure of it to a Pimms or use it in place of Benedictine in a cocktail. As the beech leaves and brandy make the finished drink quite dark, it's possible to use slightly healthier alternatives to white sugar in the recipe.

The real pleasure for me in creating this noyau is collecting the very young beech leaves as they start to unfurl in early spring—it is such a lovely, meditative thing to do. The leaves need to be a really bright green. Try to collect them from a number of different trees to prevent one tree from being stripped.

Wild Cherry BITTERS

This recipe contains a combination of foraged and online-sourced ingredients. Those I was able to collect myself were: herb bennet root, which is a bit clove-like; yarrow, which tastes vaguely of lavender; milk thistle, extremely bitter but very good for the liver; hogweed, a bit lemony and a good substitute for cardamom; and the linden nuts and blossom, which, when combined, have a chocolaty taste. Try these bitters in a Wild Cherry Manhattan (see page 162).

1 tsp gentian root

½ tsp wild cherry bark

¼ tsp milk thistle seed

1 herb bennet (*Geum urbanum*) root

1 cup (250ml) rye whiskey

1 whole star anise

½ tsp wild angelica seeds

5 hogweed (*Heracleum sphondylium*) seeds, crushed

1 tbsp lemongrass, cut into small pieces

1 vanilla bean (pod), split and scraped

4 yarrow (*Achillea millefolium*) leaves

1 cup (250ml) vodka

2 young linden (*Tilia* × *europaea* or *T. americana*) nuts, crushed

5 linden (*Tilia* × *europaea* or *T. americana*) blossoms

1 cup (200g) wild dried sour cherries or 2 cups (400g) fresh sour cherries

1½–2 cups (355–500ml) bourbon, 80 proof/40% ABV

3 x small, sealable glass jars (as used for jellies and jams), sterilized (see page 33)

Labels, to identify the jars

1-quart (1-liter) wide-mouthed, sealable jar, sterilized (see page 33)

Small, sealable presentation bottle, sterilized (see page 33)

Makes approximately ¾ pint (375ml)

> You don't actually need all the ingredients listed, so have fun experimenting. Find out what grows near you and go foraging with an expert to see what you can collect as substitutes for the bitter and aromatic ingredients.

Cut the bittering and spice ingredients, as necessary, to fit the small jars.

Put the gentian root, wild cherry bark, milk thistle seed, and herb bennet root in a small, sterilized jar and cover with the rye whiskey. Seal and label as Jar 1. Leave for 5 days, shaking the jar gently once each day. On the sixth day, strain the liquid into a wide-mouthed pitcher, then pour back into the cleaned jar and seal.

Put the star anise, angelica seeds, hogweed seeds, lemongrass, vanilla bean, and yarrow leaves in a small, sterilized jar and cover with three-quarters of the vodka. Seal and label as Jar 2. Leave for 7 days, shaking the jar gently once each day. On the eighth day, strain the liquid into the wide-mouthed pitcher, then pour back into the cleaned jar and seal.

Put the crushed linden nuts and blossoms in a small, sterilized jar, cover with the remaining vodka or as much as is needed to cover them completely. Seal and label as Jar 3. Shake gently. After 3 days, strain the liquid into the wide-mouthed pitcher, then pour back into the cleaned jar and seal.

Put the cherries in the large, sterilized jar and pour in enough bourbon to cover them (If you are using fresh cherries, you will need more bourbon). Seal and label as Jar 4. Leave for 2 weeks, shaking the jar gently once each day.

After 2 weeks, double-strain Jar 1 by pouring the contents through the fine sieve into the wide-mouthed pitcher to remove the larger solids.

Then strain again, into the cleaned jar, to get the liquid as clear as possible. Repeat for Jar 2.

If the crushed linden nuts and blossoms in Jar 3 smell vaguely chocolaty and show no signs of deterioration (they are notoriously capable of going bad), double-strain in the same way. Otherwise, discard and forget about them.

Pour the strained liquid from Jars 1, 2, and 3 (if appropriate) into Jar 4 (cherries in bourbon). Seal the jar, shake it, and leave for another 10 days.

Double-strain Jar 4, as above, first removing the cherries. Taste. If you would like a touch of sweetness, you could add a drop or two of Stevia Syrup (see page 69) or Simple Syrup (see page 68). Alternatively, keep it bitter and adjust for sweetness at the time of making your drinks.

Funnel the bitters into the presentation bottle, seal, and keep unrefrigerated for up to a year.

THE ACID TEST

Although acidity wasn't a component of cocktails originally, our palates now demand that the sweetness in a cocktail is balanced with something sour. The desire for savory cocktails is on the increase, and acidity provides a satisfying level of savoriness, which, in turn, leaves us wanting another sip.

Acidity is usually provided as citric acid, which exists in different intensities in citrus fruit such as lemons, limes, grapefruit, oranges, bergamots, and yuzu. It can also come in the form of malic acid, which is found in tree fruit like apples and pears. However, unless it's unripe, tree fruit also tends to have high concentrations of sugar, which weakens the effect of its acidity in the cocktail. Milk, wine, and vinegar also provide acidity.

The use of vinegar in cocktails was common in the 18th century, then fell out of fashion, but now it is the hallmark of a cool bar. Vinegar has been used in the past both out of necessity, to preserve fruits, and out of desire, to create stimulating punches with a concentrated burst of flavor. We have been experimenting with shrubs at Midnight Apothecary, which are essentially a fruit-based syrup with vinegar added. The word "shrub" has nothing to do with the plant. It is derived from the Arabic, *sharab*, which means "to drink."

The benefit of a shrub, apart from the burst of concentrated flavor it provides, is that, unlike bitters, it is clear, which means it is great as a mixer. As you would expect, there is much discussion among mixologists about whether to create shrubs using a hot or a cold process. To my mind, there is something undeniably magical about the cold process, which involves putting equal amounts of plant matter and some sugar under a towel in a bowl, leaving them to it, and returning a couple of days later to find a beautifully clear, bright, and potent liquid. There is a bit of science involving microorganisms too but, in practice, I find this method super-easy and superior in terms of the flavor achieved.

The tart, dry, appetite-stimulating concentration of flavor you get from combining plant matter (anything from artichokes, mint, and cucumber to cherries and kale) with sugar and vinegar does explain the resurgence of shrubs. Shrubs are more versatile and sophisticated than straight sodas (flavored soft drinks) in savory cocktails. I tend to use a good-quality, twice-fermented hard cider, champagne, or red wine vinegar, depending on the flavors of the other ingredients. The Raspberry and Scented Geranium Shrub (opposite) works beautifully in the Raspberry and Scented Geranium Sour (see pages 140–41) and, like all shrubs, should be used very sparingly. Play around with combinations of fruit and herbs to create your own perfect shrub.

Raspberry and
SCENTED GERANIUM SHRUB

All you need for this recipe, apart from your ingredients, is a tiny bit of patience and a spare surface in your kitchen to let the macerating fruit and leaves do their magic with the sugar.

18oz (500g) very ripe raspberries, washed

10 scented geranium (*Pelargonium*) leaves

4 cups (800g) superfine (caster) sugar

Approximately 2 cups (500ml) champagne vinegar or apple cider vinegar

Sealable presentation bottle(s), sterilized (see page 33)

Makes very approximately 1 pint (500ml)

Place the raspberries in a large bowl. Smack the unwashed scented geranium leaves between your palms to release the essential oils, and place them among the raspberries. Cover them with the sugar. Drape a clean dishtowel over the top of the bowl and leave on a countertop.

The maceration will take up to 48 hours—you will notice the sugar turn red, and under the crust an amazing bright raspberry liquid will appear. Strain the liquid into a measuring cup. Add an equal amount of champagne vinegar or apple cider vinegar to the amount of liquid in the measuring cup. Stir to make sure all the sugar in the liquid has dissolved. Funnel into the sterilized presentation bottle(s) and seal. This shrub will mellow with time, so try to leave it for a week before consuming. Store in the refrigerator once opened and consume within 6 months.

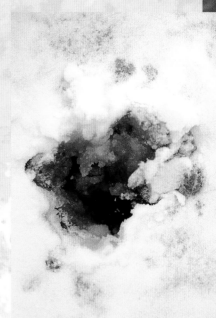

Tomato WATER

Making this recipe looks faintly macabre but the liquid created, tasting of pure, rich tomato juice, is worth the lengthy process. Used in a cocktail, this almost clear, savory liquid will reveal the other ingredients in the glass, which, of course, would not be possible with an opaque tomato juice.

To get the liquid as clear as possible, you really need to strain it through about eight layers of cheesecloth. If you have a stainless-steel chinois with a fine mesh, use that as well. You are aiming for about one drop of liquid per second, so don't expect instant results. The type and ripeness of the tomatoes will determine the final quantity you end up making.

2¼ pounds (1kg) very or slightly overripe tomatoes

1 tsp sea salt

Large square (at least 5 x 5ft/1.5 x 1.5m) of clean muslin or cheesecloth

Sealable presentation bottle(s), sterilized (see page 33)

Makes 1–2 pints (500ml–1 liter)

Wash, core, and quarter the tomatoes. Add them to the blender with the salt. Purée until smooth.

Fold the cheesecloth or muslin to create eight layers, and line a large bowl with it. Tip the purée into the center of the cheesecloth, gather the sides together to make a big pouch, and tie up tightly with string. If there is room in the refrigerator, hang the cheesecloth from above the bowl with another length of string to allow the mix to fall drop by drop into the bowl. Otherwise, use a jelly bag or a stainless-steel chinois secured over the bowl to hold the muslin.

The tomato mix needs to do its thing for up to 12 hours, so just improvise to make sure it is as secure and as cool as possible for the duration of the process. If there is more than a faint hint of tomato color in the liquid, re-strain through more layers of muslin until you get the desired clarity. Once complete, strain into the sterilized sealed bottle and refrigerate for up to 5 days.

> Use overripe tomatoes from your own vegetable garden, or you may find some at a farmers' market—sometimes traders will have a few older tomatoes that they can't sell that will be perfect for this.

Crab Apple VERJUICE

Crab apples, the unpromising fruits of *Malus sylvestris*, found in hedgerows as well as on street corners, yield a beautiful syrup and are the perfect acidifying agent for some foraged cocktails, like the Hedgerow Sour (see page 157). It's their very sourness, which makes crab apples so inedible raw, that is the clue to their success—they are packed with malic acid, which can be used in place of citric acid to make verjuice. Crab Apple Verjuice contains only half the acidity of lemon juice and is much sweeter, so you do need to use it carefully.

2¼ pounds (1kg) crab apples (ripe enough so their seeds are black)
Enough water to cover the crab apples
1 tbsp vodka, 80 proof/ 40% ABV (optional)

Food processor or blender
Several layers of muslin or a jelly bag with weights (see page 26) or an apple press or potato ricer
Sealable presentation bottle, sterilized (see page 33)

Makes approximately 1½ cups (355ml)

> Verjuice has been used since medieval times to provide acidity in cooking. Traditionally made from the pressed juice of unripe grapes, crab apples took their place where grapes were not available. Unripe gooseberries and wild plums produce something similar.

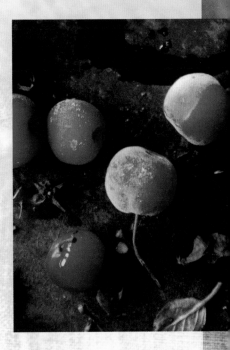

Wash the apples but do not cut them. Pour enough water into a large, nonreactive pan to cover the apples and bring to a rolling boil. Add the apples whole, bring back to a boil, and blanch for 1 minute—this makes the fruit softer and easier to press. Remove from the heat and run under cold water.

Add the crab apples in batches to the food processor or blender and blitz them to a pulp. If they are particularly large apples, you may need to halve them. Strain the pulped mix into a large, wide-mouthed pitcher through a fine-mesh sieve lined with several layers of cheesecloth or a jelly bag, and weighed down with something heavy (like cans of food) to extract the juice. Alternatively, use an apple press or a potato ricer.

Funnel the juice into the sterilized presentation bottle and seal, adding 1 tablespoon of high-proof alcohol if you want to preserve the verjuice. If you don't add any alcohol, the sugars and yeast are likely to ferment. It is OK to let this happen over a couple of days (some people prefer to do this anyway) and then add the alcohol to stop the fermentation process. Store in a cool, dark place for up to a year. Once opened, use within a month.

Oleo SACCHARUM

Don't thank me for this recipe, thank David Wondrich, author of *Punch: The Delights (and Dangers) of the Flowing Bowl*. He maintains, and now I must concur, that the secret to a good punch is oleo saccharum, which translates as "oily sugar." But it's capable of doing so much more. It turns out that oleo saccharum works perfectly in a whole host of individual drinks and was commonly used in the 19th century by bartenders for that purpose.

Start off with citrus and sugar—Wondrich suggests lemon for the citrus element, but you can play around with other citrus fruits, as well as different types of sugar, and any herbs you may want to add. I've used a mix of oranges, bergamot, and lemon with rosemary, scented geranium, and French tarragon.

2 unwaxed, organic oranges (see page 15)

2 unwaxed, organic lemons (see page 15)

2 unwaxed, organic bergamots (see page 48)

5 scented geranium (*Pelargonium*) leaves

2 sprigs rosemary

1 sprig French tarragon

1 cup (200g) superfine (caster) sugar

Makes approximately ¼ pint (125ml)

Zest the oranges, lemons, and bergamots with a vegetable peeler, and place in a bowl. Add the unwashed geranium leaves, herbs, and sugar. Mix everything together with your hands, then muddle using a muddler or the end of a wooden spoon to release all those wondrous oils. Cover with plastic wrap, lest the oils escape!

Leave for at least an hour, preferably two, coming back perhaps twice to give another little muddle and maybe add a bit more sugar. You will be left with exactly what it says: a sugary oil. Yum. Use immediately.

BLOOD ORANGE, GRAPEFRUIT, AND ROSEMARY OLEO SACCHARUM

This stunning variation is used in a Wild Bloody Rosemary (see page 165). Substitute 3 blood oranges for the regular oranges, and 2 grapefruits for the lemons and bergamots. Instead of 2 sprigs of rosemary, use 4, and omit the scented geranium leaves and tarragon.

As well as being the base of many a cocktail, this oily elixir can be mixed with a little water, heated, combined with the juice of the citrus you've zested, and turned into a fantastic lemonade.

CHAPTER 3

THE RECIPES

These cocktails are divided into garden, foraged, restorative, and nonalcoholic. If you don't grow the fresh ingredients yourself, most of them can be found in markets or stores, or substituted with similar fresh ingredients. Foraged cocktails use ingredients you can find growing in the wild but, again, you can often buy them or find substitutes. The restorative cocktails are there for when you need a specific "pick-me-up" (not all are nonalcoholic), and the nonalcoholic ones speak for themselves. Play around, taste-test, substitute, cheat. The idea is to complement and enhance, not obscure, already delicious liquors, and to create great cocktails. The pleasure principle is the driving force, but a bit of balance and measuring will make all the difference.

GARDEN COCKTAILS

These cocktails are bursting with ingredients that can be grown in your back yard, windowsill, or community garden. Don't worry if you don't have the space. Most can also be sourced at local farmers' markets and stores selling vibrant, organic vegetables, herbs, and flowers. Cocktails are a feast for the senses, and their aroma alone can conjure up powerful emotions. Whether it's a childhood summer meadow (try the Field of Dreams, page 126) or a magical summer evening (the Chelsea Fringe Collins, page 116), I hope you have fun experimenting. These recipes are a good place to start if you would like some structure and balance!

Lavender BEE'S KNEES

This is a take on a classic Prohibition-era cocktail of gin, honey, and lemon juice. Initially, it was created to mask the dubious quality of the liquor of the day. This version brings the glorious lavender-infused gin to the fore, with the honey and lavender working extremely well together.

2oz (60ml) Lavender Gin (see page 47)
¾oz (22ml) Honey Simple Syrup (see page 69)
½oz (15ml) freshly squeezed lemon juice

Tools: **Cocktail shaker with strainer**
Glass: **Martini**
Ice: **Cubes**
Garnish: **Lavender sprig**

Serves 1

Add all the ingredients to the cocktail shaker and fill it two-thirds of the way up with ice. Cover and shake hard for 20 seconds, then strain the contents of the shaker into the glass. Garnish with the sprig of lavender.

The type of honey and where it was produced will affect the taste, so, although you may use exactly the same proportions, your Lavender Bee's Knees will taste different from mine. But it should still be delicious.

Bacon and Garlic
OLD FASHIONED

This truly savory cocktail makes good use of the Bacon and Tea, Smoke-infused Whisky recipe (see page 39). When I first made it, I wanted to be a bit playful with the garlic chives that were in flower in the garden but without overpowering the drink with a garlic flavor. The solution was to make a large ice sphere or ice cube with a garlic chive flower inside for each drink.

1 barspoon (1 tsp) Rich Simple Syrup (see page 68)

3 dashes of angostura bitters

2oz (60ml) Bacon and Tea, Smoke-infused Whisky (see page 39), or just Scotch or bourbon

Tools: **Barspoon/teaspoon, ice sphere maker**

Glass: **Rocks**

Ice/Garnish: **Large ice sphere/cube, with garlic chive flower inside (see page 32)**

Serves 1

Pour the Rich Simple Syrup into the glass. Add the angostura bitters. Stir to combine the syrup and bitters, and line the whole of the bottom of the glass. Place the garlic chive flower ice sphere or cube in the glass. Pour over the smoke-infused whisky. Stir to chill the drink. Serve immediately.

As the ice melts, the drink is very mildly infused with a tang of garlic, and the flower looks like a fossilized plant trapped in amber.

Chocolate
MINT JULEP

In this recipe, the spicy mint pairs perfectly with the caramel-y bourbon and, because of the syrup, you will capture more of the taste, not just the aroma, of the mint. Ideally, Chocolate Mint Julep is best served in a frozen silver or pewter julep cup but a rocks glass works just as well, as long as it is chilled in the refrigerator or freezer first.

2 chocolate mint (*Mentha × piperata* f. *citrata* 'Chocolate') sprigs (one is for the garnish)
1oz (30ml) Chocolate Mint Syrup (see page 80)
2oz (60ml) bourbon

Glass: **Rocks/julep cup**
Ice: **Crushed**
Garnish: **Chocolate mint sprig**

Serves 1

Chill the glass in the freezer for at least 30 minutes. Smack a mint leaf between your palms to release the essential oil and rub it around the edge of the chilled glass. Place the leaf and one more smacked one in the glass. Pour in the Chocolate Mint Syrup and fill the glass with ice. Add the bourbon through the ice and stir to combine and chill the drink still further. Garnish with the sprig of chocolate mint.

CACAO NIB VODKA VARIATION

To bump up the chocolaty taste as well as the aroma—and make the whole cocktail slightly less sweet— pour ½oz (15ml) of Cacao Nib Vodka (see page 49) into each glass over the crushed ice, before adding the garnish. Alternatively, add 3 dashes of chocolate bitters, available from quality liquor suppliers. You will get a slight bitterness from the cacao nib vodka, so you don't need both.

Unsurprisingly, mint is rich in menthol, an aromatic volatile responsible for producing the stimulating and warming vapor that is picked up at the back of the nose and travels straight to the brain. In Chocolate Mint Julep, that vapor is extraordinary.

CHELSEA FRINGE *Collins*

In spring 2013 I was asked to design a cocktail for The Chelsea Fringe, the alternative to the more famous Chelsea Flower Show—the annual spectacle of English eccentricity, passion, and obsession with plants and gardening. My Chelsea Fringe Collins was designed to look, taste, and smell like "summer in a glass." I wanted to capture the very intense aroma of summer evenings—and that meant jasmine, which had to permeate the gin. Essence of jasmine does the job better than I could with the amount of blossoms I would realistically have to infuse in the gin. The Rose Petal Syrup adds to the summer scent, and no English summer is complete without elderflower. The lemon juice cuts through their sweetness, while the orange bitters provides the final seasoning.

2oz (60ml) jasmine-infused Jensen Old Tom Gin

½oz (15ml) Elderflower Liqueur (see page 57)

½oz (15ml) Rose Petal Syrup (see page 75)

Dash of orange bitters

¾oz (22ml) freshly squeezed lemon juice

Soda water

Dash of cassis (optional)

Tools: **Cocktail shaker with strainer, tweezers/small tongs, pipette/barspoon (optional)**

Glass: **Collins**

Ice: **Cubes**

Garnish: **Borage flowers, wild strawberries, wild fennel fronds, lavender sprig, dianthus petals, lemon twist**

Serves 1

Fill the glass with ice. Tuck some wild strawberries, fennel fronds, the lavender sprig, borage flowers, and a few dianthus petals in among the ice cubes, sandwiched against the glass, for maximum visual impact. Save a few borage flowers for the final garnish.

Add the gin, Elderflower Liqueur, Rose Petal Syrup, orange bitters, and lemon juice to the cocktail shaker. Fill it two-thirds full with ice, cover, and shake hard for 20 seconds. Strain the mixture into the chilled glass over the ice.

Garnish with the lemon twist and remaining flowers, using the tweezers or small tongs, then top with the soda water (it is important to add the garnish before the soda water, otherwise you will push the soda water out of the glass.)

Use a pipette or the top of a barspoon to drop the cassis to the bottom of the glass to create a color contrast (optional).

JASMINE GIN

Edible flower essences are expensive but you need only a few drops per bottle of spirit. For Jasmine Gin, add 5 drops of edible-grade essence of jasmine for every 24oz (700ml) of gin.

> The visuals of this cocktail are just as important as the ingredients. Use a tall, thin glass, so you can wedge the flower garnishes between the ice and the side of the glass.

Clover CLUB

This version of the very well-known pre-Prohibition cocktail uses Raspberry and Thyme Syrup (see page 81). Raspberries work so well with gin, and when they're in season, it seems a shame not to put them in everything. The egg-white foam provides a lovely mouth-feel and body to the cocktail, and is the perfect surface for a garnish.

1 thyme sprig
1 egg white
2oz (60ml) gin
1oz (30ml) Raspberry and Thyme Syrup (see page 81)
¾oz (22ml) freshly squeezed lemon juice

Tools: **Cocktail shaker with strainer, tea strainer**
Glass: **Martini**
Ice: **Cubes**
Garnish: **Thyme sprig**

Serves 1

Smack the thyme sprig between your palms to release the essential oils and drop into the cocktail shaker. Add the egg white, cover, and dry-shake hard for 20 seconds (see page 33). (Doing this without any ice really emulsifies the egg, which will produce a great foam on top of the cocktail.) Add the remaining ingredients to the shaker and fill it two-thirds full with ice. Cover and shake hard for another 20 seconds. Double-strain (see page 29) the mixture into the glass with the tea strainer to catch any pieces of thyme. Garnish with the second sprig of thyme.

Traditionally, the Clover Club consists of gin, raspberry syrup (or grenadine, made with pomegranate), lemon juice, and an egg white. People have played around with this formula for a long time and added their own herbal variations.

LIMONCELLO *with Strawberries and Cream Foam*

This is an extravagant summer dessert cocktail. It would be too sweet and cloying if you didn't have the acidity from the lemon juice. The vodka reduces the sweetness too and increases the strength when combined with the mild cream foam, creating a very balanced, flavorsome drink.

Tools: **Cocktail shaker with strainer, non-aerosol cream whipper (see page 36)**

Glass: **Martini**

Ice: **Cubes**

Garnish: **Strawberry slice, lavender sprig**

Serves 1

1oz (30ml) vodka

¾oz (22ml) Scented Geranium and Lavender Limoncello (see page 58) or good-quality, store-bought limoncello

¾oz (22ml) freshly squeezed lemon juice

Strawberry and Cream Foam (see page 38)

Combine the vodka, limoncello, and lemon juice in the cocktail shaker. Add ice, cover the shaker, and shake hard for 20 seconds. Strain the mixture into the glass. Using the non-aerosol cream whipper (see page 36), top with the Strawberry and Cream Foam. Garnish with the slice of fresh strawberry, speared with a lavender sprig.

Lavender GIN FIZZ

Lavender adds a subtle, floral note to summer drinks. It combines particularly well with honey, citrus, and bitter flavors. I add a dash of Parfait Amour (a dark purple liqueur, flavored with rose and violet petals, vanilla beans/pods, and orange blossom) simply to intensify the lavender color.

We have clouds of lavender in the garden at Midnight Apothecary, which, as well as providing flavor in this delicious cocktail, makes a really attractive garnish.

2oz (60ml) Lavender Gin (see page 47)
¾oz (22ml) Honey Simple Syrup (see page 69)
¾oz (22ml) freshly squeezed lemon juice
Dash of Parfait Amour
Dash of orange bitters
Soda water

Fill the glass with ice. Add all the ingredients, except the soda water, to the cocktail shaker and fill it two-thirds full with ice. Cover and shake hard for 20 seconds. Strain the mixture into the chilled glass over the ice. Cut a sprig of lavender to fit just above the rim of the glass. Top with soda water. Add the straw and serve.

Tools: **Cocktail shaker with strainer, scissors**
Glass: **Collins**
Ice: **Cubes**
Garnish: **Lavender sprig, straw**

Serves 1

PEA~_Tini_

The inspiration for this recipe followed a glut of peas. People will argue that anything other than gin or vodka and a splash of dry vermouth is most certainly not a Martini, but let's not get hysterical. This cocktail fits the name and the glass. And it's delicious.

Tools: **Cocktail shaker with strainer, tea strainer**
Glass: **Martini**
Ice: **Cubes**
Garnish: **Split open pea pod, mint sprig**

Serves 1

3 mint leaves
1oz (30ml) floral gin, such as Jensen Old Tom
1oz (30ml) Pea Purée (see page 126)
¾oz (22ml) Simple Syrup (see page 68)
½oz (15ml) freshly squeezed lime juice

Chill the glass thoroughly in the freezer or refrigerator for 2 or 4 hours respectively. Alternatively, fill the glass with ice.

Smack the 3 mint leaves between your palms to release the essential oils and drop into the cocktail shaker. Add the gin, Pea Purée, Simple Syrup, and lime juice. Fill the shaker two-thirds of the way up with ice. Cover and shake hard for 20 seconds. If you used ice to chill your glass, empty it out. Double-strain (see page 29) the cocktail into the chilled glass with the tea strainer to catch the pieces of mint. Garnish with the split pea pod and sprig of mint.

Strawberry and Basil GIMLET

Strawberries and basil (*Ocimum basilicum*) are a delicious combination, and this simple cocktail allows them to take center stage. The grind of black pepper draws out the flavor of the strawberries, and put together with the aromatic, sweet, earthy basil, you'll have a smile on your face.

3 large strawberries
½oz (15ml) agave nectar
4 basil leaves
2oz (60ml) gin
½oz (15ml) freshly squeezed lime juice
Grind of coarse ground black pepper

Tools: **Cocktail shaker with strainer, tea strainer**
Glass: **Martini/wine**
Ice: **Cubes**
Garnish: **Strawberry slice, large basil leaf**
Serves 1

Put the strawberries and agave nectar in the cocktail shaker, and muddle (see page 33) thoroughly. Smack the basil leaves between your palms to release the essential oils and drop in the shaker. Add the remaining ingredients. Fill the shaker two-thirds full with ice, cover, and shake hard for 20 seconds. Double-strain (see page 29) the mixture by pouring it through the tea strainer, into the glass. Garnish with the strawberry slice and basil leaf.

Hibiscus and Blackcurrant Leaf MOJITO

The beautiful flowers of blackcurrant sage (*Salvia microphylla*) and blackcurrant leaves in the Midnight Apothecary garden in mid-summer provided the inspiration for this cocktail. I had bought some dried wild hibiscus flowers (*Hibiscus sabdariffa*) in a local Afro-Caribbean market—they are not hardy in the U.K.—but I knew the calyx (the outer whorl of the flower) is commonly used around the world to make a delicious deep red syrup (see below). As well as being very dramatic, the syrup is very high in vitamin C.

1 lime, cut into 6 wedges

5 small blackcurrant leaves, 3 whole and 2 finely sliced

1 tsp (5ml) demerara/ turbinado sugar

¾oz (22ml) Wild Hibiscus Syrup (see below)

2oz (60ml) spiced rum

Soda water

Tools: **Muddler, stirring rod**

Glass: **Collins**

Ice: **Cubes**

Garnish: **Sprig of blackcurrant sage in flower, blackcurrant leaves, and hollyhock (*Alcea*) flower**

Serves 1

Put 4 wedges of lime, 3 whole blackcurrant leaves, and the sugar in the glass, and muddle (see page 33). Add the Wild Hibiscus Syrup. Half-fill the glass with ice. Add the rum, the remaining 2 lime wedges, and the 2 finely sliced blackcurrant leaves. Top with soda water and serve with a stirring rod (straw or spoon if not!). Garnish with the sprig of blackcurrant sage flowers and blackcurrant leaves. You could add a hollyhock flower, too.

WILD HIBISCUS SYRUP

Add equal volumes of dried flowers, sugar, and water—for example, 1 cup of flowers, 1 cup of superfine (caster) sugar, and 1 cup of water—to a nonreactive pan and bring to a boil. Remove from the heat and let the ingredients steep for 20 minutes. Strain (see page 29), reserving the calyx (flower) as a garnish.

Wild hibiscus flowers are sometimes used in high-end cocktail bars to garnish Bellinis—the flower head is the perfect size to nestle in the base of a champagne flute.

Traditionally, a mojito is muddled mint, rum, simple syrup, and lime juice, topped up with soda water, but you can experiment to your heart's desire with variations on this theme, according to whichever herbs and fruit are in season.

Field of Dreams (EGG & PEAS!)

This cocktail came about by happy accident, following a glut of peas. I wanted to represent a field bursting with meadow flowers: the green grass was easy to replicate with the peas, and the flower garnish needed a white foam to rest on, so that required egg... hence this cocktail's other name. For the garnish, use whatever edible flowers are around at the time of making.

Tools: **Cocktail shaker with strainer**
Glass: **Highball/tumbler**
Ice: **Cubes**
Garnish: **Edible flowers, such as oxeye daisies, cornflowers, wild vetch sprig (do NOT eat more than one sprig of wild vetch, as they are toxic in large doses).**

Serves 1

4 mint leaves, preferably spearmint (*Mentha spicata*)
Dash of Elderflower Liqueur (see page 57)
1 egg white
¾oz (22ml) Kamm & Sons (see below)
¾oz (22ml) floral gin, such as Jensen Old Tom
2oz (60ml) Pea Purée (see below)
2 tsp (10ml) freshly squeezed lemon juice

Smack the mint leaves between your palms and drop into the cocktail shaker. Add the Elderflower Liqueur and the egg white. Cover the shaker and dry-shake hard for 20 seconds (see page 33). Add the remaining ingredients and fill the shaker two-thirds of the way up with ice. Cover again and shake hard for another 20 seconds. Double-strain (see page 29) the mixture into the glass, using the tea strainer to catch any mint solids. Place your edible flowers on the foam and serve immediately.

PEA PURÉE

Mix ¼ cup (60g) of fresh or thawed frozen small peas with just enough water to liquefy the peas in a blender. Pulse for a few seconds, then turn up to high for 15 seconds. Strain through a fine mesh to ensure that the purée is smooth.

Kamm & Sons is an exquisite, small-batch apéritif made with ginseng, manuka honey, and about 45 botanicals in total. It is slightly bitter but has strong honey and citrus notes.

Pear and Lavender HEAVEN

This is a floral delight for the taste buds and not bad to look at either. Lavender and pears work really well together. If you don't have pear purée, pear juice will work fine. And if you have no Meadowsweet Syrup, you could always use elderflower cordial or syrup.

4 basil leaves
½oz (15ml) Meadowsweet Syrup (see page 86)
2oz (60ml) Lavender Gin (see page 47)
1oz (30ml) organic pear purée
½oz (15ml) freshly squeezed lemon juice

Tools: **Cocktail shaker with strainer, tea strainer**
Glass: **Martini**
Ice: **Cubes**
Garnish: **Lavender sprig, slice of lemon zest**

Serves 1

Chill the glass thoroughly in the freezer or refrigerator for 2 or 4 hours respectively. Alternatively, fill the glass with ice.

Smack the basil leaves between your palms to release the essential oils and drop into the cocktail shaker. Add the remaining ingredients. Fill the shaker two-thirds of the way up with ice, cover, and shake hard for 20 seconds. If you used ice to chill your glass, empty it out. Double-strain the cocktail (see page 29) into the chilled glass with the tea strainer. Garnish with the sprig of lavender and lemon zest.

Jam BELLINI

This is the easiest cocktail to make, using whichever fruit is in season, yet it is also quite decadent because of the bubbles. I make it with prosecco but any sparkling wine will do, as long as it is dry to counteract the sweetness of the Blackberry Purée. You can have fun serving these Bellinis in different vessels. Try a jam jar or Mason jar, with a straw for a casual, summertime look.

3 tbsp (45ml) Blackberry Purée (see below)

4oz (125ml) prosecco or other dry sparkling wine, chilled

Tools: **Barspoon, toothpick (cocktail stick)**

Glass: **Champagne flute or glass jar**

Garnish: **3 blackberries on a toothpick**

Serves 1

Pour the purée carefully into the glass. Slowly add the sparkling wine, stirring as you do to combine the purée with the bubbly. Garnish with the blackberries on the toothpick (cocktail stick).

BLACKBERRY PURÉE

Take 2 cups (250g) of very ripe blackberries and place in a blender with 2 tablespoons (30ml) of lemon juice and ¼ cup (60ml) of Simple Syrup (see page 68). If you don't have a blender, place 2 cups (250g) of very ripe berries in a small, nonreactive pan with 2 tablespoons (30ml) of lemon juice, ¼ cup (60g) of superfine (caster) sugar, and 2 tablespoons (30ml) of water. Heat slowly until the sugar has dissolved. Whichever method you use, you MUST then strain the mixture through a fine-mesh strainer (see page 26) to remove any pips and ensure the purée is smooth. Once made, store in the refrigerator and use within a couple of days. This recipe makes about 5 servings.

SUMMER BERRY PURÉE

Raspberries and redcurrants also make excellent purées for a Bellini. Simply use the same amount of fruit as in the Blackberry Purée recipe. Alternatively, use a mix of blackberries, raspberries, and redcurrants.

Any leftover compote from the Rhubarb and Ginger Syrup (see page 79) is another ready-made substitute for a Bellini. There's no need to add anything—just blend and strain it to make sure that it is smooth.

TARRAGON AND APRICOT
Caipirinha

We aren't able to grow apricots at Midnight Apothecary but the local markets burgeon with the most delicious, sweet, and juicy ones in summer. They marry so well with French tarragon (*Artemisia dracunculus sativa*), which we do grow, that we made this caipirinha in honor of the Soccer World Cup finals held in Brazil in 2014. This take on the country's national drink is a rough-and-ready cocktail that includes chunks of apricot.

Tools: **Cocktail shaker, muddler**
Glass: **Tumbler/rocks**
Ice: **Cracked (see page 32)**
Garnish: **2 apricot wedges, tarragon sprig**

Serves 1

1 apricot, cut into 6 wedges (save 2 for garnish)
1 lime, cut into 4 wedges
¾oz (22ml) agave nectar
1 French tarragon sprig
2oz (60ml) cachaça

Place 4 apricot wedges and the lime wedges in the cocktail shaker. Pour in the agave nectar, and muddle thoroughly (see page 33). Smack the tarragon sprig between your palms to release its essential oils and add to the mix. Add the cachaça and a couple of handfuls of cracked ice. Cover and shake hard for 20 seconds. Pour (but do not strain) the mixture into the glass. Remove the shaken tarragon sprig. Garnish with a fresh sprig, to keep up appearances, and 2 apricot wedges.

We use French tarragon in this recipe, as it is much more pungent, sweet, and aromatic than Russian tarragon.

Rhubarbra COLLINS

This is such a popular drink at Midnight Apothecary. Rhubarb and ginger are a very pleasing combination, and the color of the drink is particularly beautiful if you can find the really red stalks of rhubarb for the syrup. An Alexanders stalk (*Angelica atropurpurea*) is used as a swizzle stick in place of a rhubarb stalk because it has a pleasant anise/celery taste, as opposed to the impossibly tart taste of raw rhubarb. It is also very interesting to look at. The anise flavor is reflected in the fennel-infused gin, which pairs up perfectly with the rhubarb and ginger. A shard of very fresh ginger will also make a great swizzle stick.

2oz (60ml) Fennel-infused Gin (see page 53)

1oz (30ml) Rhubarb and Ginger Syrup (see page 79)

1oz (30ml) freshly squeezed lemon juice

Soda water

Tools: **Cocktail shaker with strainer**
Glass: **Collins**
Ice: **Cubes**
Garnish: **Alexanders swizzle stick, straw**

Serves 1

Fill the glass with ice. Combine all the ingredients in the cocktail shaker and fill it two-thirds of the way up with ice. Cover and shake hard for 20 seconds. Strain the mixture into the glass over the ice. Add the swizzle stick and straw. Top up with soda water and serve.

Alexanders grow everywhere, from shady wasteland to woodland, and they are very difficult to confuse with anything poisonous.

Grilled Nectarine
SMASH

With its cozy firepits and giant candles, Midnight Apothecary is synonymous with fire, so, come the summer, it's natural for us to barbecue fruit for our cocktails. The natural sugars of fruit and citrus caramelize beautifully for a slightly charred, smoky sweetness. Nectarines, peaches, and cherries are perfect for this, as are lemons and limes. We use a barrel-aged cachaça for its smoky aroma, which adds to the whole fire theme.

1 nectarine, halved, with the pit (stone) removed (save a thin wedge for the garnish)
1 lime, sliced into 4 wheels
1 thyme sprig
¼oz (7ml) Simple Syrup (see page 68)
2oz (60ml) cachaça

Tools: **Grill (barbecue), tongs, muddler**
Glass: **Rocks**
Ice: **Crushed (see page 32)**
Garnish: **Thyme sprig, nectarine wedge**

Serves 1

Place the nectarine halves and lime wheels on a hot grill (barbecue) and wait for the sugars in them to start to bubble and char. Turn the fruits over and repeat on the other side—the whole process should take around 5 minutes. Remove from the heat and let cool (another 10 minutes).

Muddle (see page 33) the nectarines, lime wheels, and 1 sprig of thyme in the sugar syrup at the bottom of the glass. Add crushed ice almost to the brim. Pour the cachaça through the ice and stir. Garnish with another sprig of thyme and a thin wedge of nectarine.

COCKTAIL VARIATIONS

Nectarines and brandy go really well together, so you could replace the cachaça with brandy or, indeed, an aged rum, and use lemon instead of the lime.

Strawberry Lemony
HEAVEN

Strawberries and thyme work wonderfully together, and we had loads of both growing in the garden this summer. This is an extremely simple, unfussy cocktail, and it's hard to beat the refreshing taste of strawberries, thyme, and lemon juice as a summer flavor combination. You can extract the juice and flavor of strawberries simply by muddling really ripe ones into some Thyme Syrup and letting them sit for about 30 minutes to macerate very slightly. The freshness of the strawberries shines through spectacularly. Instead of Thyme Syrup, try fresh thyme and Simple Syrup.

2 sprigs of lemon thyme, about 4in (10cm) long (only if you haven't made Thyme Syrup)

2 large strawberries or 3 medium strawberries, washed and sliced

1oz (30ml) Thyme Syrup (see page 80) or Simple Syrup (see page 68)

2oz (60ml) white rum, vodka, or gin

¾oz (22ml) freshly squeezed lemon juice

Soda water

Tools: **Muddler, cocktail shaker with strainer**
Glass: **Collins**
Ice: **Cubes**
Garnish: **Lemon thyme sprig, sliced strawberry, lemon wheel, straw**

Serves 1

Fill the glass with ice. If you haven't made Thyme Syrup, smack 2 fresh sprigs of thyme between your palms to release the essential oils. Drop into the cocktail shaker with a dash of Simple Syrup.

If you have made Thyme Syrup, skip the step above and instead muddle (see page 33) the strawberry slices really thoroughly with a dash of the Thyme Syrup in the shaker, to release all the strawberry juice. (You can do this 30 minutes ahead of time to let the sugar syrup extract even more juice, but it's not essential.)

For those of you using fresh thyme: add your strawberries now and muddle as above. For both methods, pour the rest of the Thyme/Simple Syrup and your remaining ingredients (except the soda water) into the shaker. Fill it two-thirds of the way up with ice, cover, and shake hard for 20 seconds. Strain the mixture into the glass of ice—don't worry about tiny bits of thyme; they look attractive. Garnish with a fresh sprig of lemon thyme, strawberry slices, and a lemon wheel. Add the soda water and a straw.

Whether you use white rum, vodka, or gin to provide the kick is entirely up to you.

Pretty in PINK

Rhubarb and roses are a winner together, people, with the tartness of the rhubarb, and the floral sweetness of the roses. This cocktail is a riff on the classic Ramos Gin Fizz, invented by Mr. Henry C. Ramos in New Orleans in the 1880s. I use rose-petal infused gin and rose water (you can buy bottles in supermarkets or Middle Eastern stores) in place of orange flower water, and I add a little Rose Petal Syrup with the rhubarb syrup to provide extra floral notes to this baby-pink, creamy drink. It's divine.

2oz (60ml) Rose Petal Gin (see page 46)

Dash of rose water

½oz (15ml) heavy (double) cream

½oz (15ml) freshly squeezed lemon juice

½oz (15ml) freshly squeezed lime juice

½oz (15ml) Rhubarb Syrup (see page 79, but omit the ginger)

1 tsp (5ml) Rose Petal Syrup (see page 75)

1 large egg white

1oz (30ml) soda water

Tools: **Cocktail shaker with strainer**

Glass: **Collins**

Ice: **Cubes**

Garnish: **Rosebud/rose petal**

Serves 1

Combine all the ingredients (except the ice, soda water, and rose garnish) in the cocktail shaker. Cover and shake hard for at least 25 seconds to really emulsify the egg and marry the different consistencies thoroughly. Fill the shaker two-thirds of the way up with ice. Cover again and shake hard for at least another 20 seconds. Strain the mixture into the glass. Pour the soda water into the shaker to loosen any remaining froth, then gently pour into the glass to form extra foam on top of the cocktail. Garnish with a rosebud or rose petal.

Salad DAYS

This is taking salad options in liquid form to cocktail land. The trick is to make the tomato water as clear as possible, so that you are staring into a beautiful rock pool of contrasting colors rather than a sludgy mess. The aged balsamic vinegar provides the umami, savory, acidic note that's needed to accompany the tomato water, but it is mellow and provides you with a satisfying urge to have another sip. I use the pungent and pretty micro-shoots of leaves that have just sprouted, like red amaranth (*Amaranthus cruentus*), as well as larger, more mature leaves with even more flavor, such as basil (*Ocimum basilicum*), cut into very thin strips.

A salt rim isn't absolutely necessary but if you have some pink salt, which I've used here, or black or even regular sea salt, it adds another layer of texture, color, and savoriness.

As with a regular salad, play around with the salad leaves for color and taste. The greens, reds, and purples of the different leaves and the tomatoes will provide the contrasting colors and tastes you are looking for.

1 lemon wedge and 1 tbsp (20g) pink salt, for rim
1 large purple basil leaf
1 large green basil leaf
2oz (60ml) vodka
1½oz (45ml) Tomato Water (see page 106)
½oz (15ml) freshly squeezed lime juice
Dash of aged balsamic vinegar
3 red and 3 yellow cherry tomatoes, halved
Pinch of salt and freshly ground black pepper
6 micro-shoots of red amaranth, cut into very thin strips

Tools: **Cocktail shaker**
Glass: **Collins**
Ice: **Cubes**
Garnish: **2 purple and 2 green basil leaves, cut into very thin strips**

Serves 1

Rub the lemon wedge around one half of the exterior rim of the glass (see page 35) and shake off any excess juice. Dip that half of the outside edge of the glass into the pink salt to coat it. Shake off any excess.

Smack the 2 basil leaves between your palms to release the essential oils and drop into the cocktail shaker. Add the vodka, Tomato Water, lime juice, balsamic vinegar, halved cherry tomatoes, and salt and pepper. Fill the shaker two-thirds of the way up with ice. Cover and shake hard for 20 seconds. Add the micro-shoots of red amaranth. Pour (do not strain) the mixture, including the ice, into the glass and stir in the remaining basil leaves. Serve immediately.

Purple FIRE AND ICE

I have been playing around with beetroot in cocktails for a while now and wanted a liquor to go with it that would reflect its earthiness. I thought an aged Reposado tequila, with its intense agave scent, might provide just that. However, I got hold of an aged mescal instead, which is distilled from the fire-roasted heart of the agave, as opposed to the steamed heart of blue agave used to make tequila. The campfire smokiness in the mescal was perfect.

Pomegranate molasses, available from many large grocery stores and Middle Eastern and Mediterranean food stores, gave just the right level of fragrant, tangy sweetness and another level of richness to stand up to the campfire taste of the mescal. I squeezed a tiny amount of juice from some grated fresh ginger just because I thought it would go well with all the other ingredients.

1½oz (45ml) aged Reposado mescal

1oz (30ml) beetroot juice (either store-bought or juice your own)

½oz (15ml) pomegranate molasses

¾oz (22ml) freshly squeezed lime juice

1 tsp (5ml) fresh ginger juice

1 scoop ice cream (see box, right)

Tools: **Cocktail shaker with strainer, ice cream scoop**

Glass: **Champagne coupe/ small glass bowl**

Ice: **Cubes**

Garnish: **Anise hyssop (*Agastache foeniculum*) flower**

Serves 1

Add all the ingredients (apart from the ice cream and garnish) to the cocktail shaker. Fill it two-thirds of the way up with ice. Cover and shake hard for 20 seconds. Dip the ice cream scoop in hot water and scoop out a ball of ice cream. Place in the center of the glass. Strain the cocktail into the glass. Push the stem of the anise hyssop flower into the ice cream as garnish. Serve with 1 or 2 spoons or straws, depending on how romantic you want to be!

You can use any sweet-flavored ice cream to counteract the other ingredients. I use elderflower and gooseberry which gives a complete contrast in taste and color, and provides an air of decadence. A delicious alternative would be ginger ice cream.

The beautiful lavender-blue flower of anise hyssop, with its vaguely minty, licorice scent, is the perfect garnish.

Raspberry &
SCENTED GERANIUM SOUR

This very pretty, delicious, pink cocktail is a riff on raspberries and lemon treated in various ways, with an extra layer of depth provided by the use of scented geraniums (*Pelargonium*) and vinegar. Although you can't taste it directly, the vinegar in the Shrub gives a savory umami depth, which is rounded off with a dash of angostura bitters. The frothy body of the egg-white foam provides a mildness and beautiful mouth-feel in contrast to the strong, punchy gold rum, creating a very balanced, luxurious cocktail.

Rub and sniff the scented geranium leaf in the garnish before drinking to release the essential oils and stimulate the taste buds.

The garnish of three little flowers provides pleasure for the eyes to ensure that no sense is left unsated! Top candidates for this are the exquisite flowers of plants from the mint (Lamiaceae) or borage (Boraginaceae) family, such as rosemary or viper's bugloss.

1oz (30ml) Scented Geranium Vodka (see page 52)

1oz (30ml) gold rum

¾oz (22ml) Lemon Verbena and Raspberry Syrup (see page 81)

2 tsp (10ml) Raspberry and Scented Geranium Shrub (see page 105)

2 tsp (10ml) freshly squeezed lemon juice

1 egg white

Dash of angostura bitters

Tools: **Cocktail shaker with strainer, tweezers (optional)**

Glass: **Martini**

Ice: **Cubes**

Garnish: **Scented geranium (*Pelargonium*) leaf, 3 tiny edible flowers, such as rosemary or viper's bugloss (*Echium vulgare*)**

Chill the glass thoroughly in the freezer or refrigerator for 2 or 4 hours respectively. Alternatively, fill the glass with ice.

Pour all the ingredients (but no ice) into the cocktail shaker. Cover and dry-shake hard for 20 seconds (see page 33) to consolidate all the ingredients and really emulsify the egg white. Add ice to the shaker, cover again, and shake hard for another 20 seconds. If you used ice to chill your glass, empty it out. Strain the cocktail into the chilled glass. Let the egg-white foam settle. Place the scented geranium leaf and the 3 edible flowers on top of the foam, using tweezers if necessary, and then serve.

Serves 1

Shiso MARTINI

Shiso or Japanese basil (*Perilla frutescens*) is a beautiful garden plant from the mint family that will bring joy to all your senses. Its bright green or purple, furry, frilly leaves make quite a statement in your herb patch, and their anise, citrusy, minty, aromatic taste gives a wonderful astringency to a cocktail. This very simple, dry Martini is meant to evoke the tranquillity of a Japanese garden, but I couldn't help but "big up" the oriental element during Midnight Apothecary's Japanese celebrations by adding some zest from the Japanese yuzu fruit, so it's not even a Martini in the strictest sense—just dry, aromatic, and delicious.

Tools: **Mixing glass, muddler, barspoon/stirring rod, hawthorne strainer, tea strainer**

Glass: **Martini**

Ice: **Cubes**

Garnish: **Shiso leaf**

Serves 1

Dash of yuzu juice or zest of ½ yuzu
3 purple or 3 green shiso leaves
2oz (60ml) gin or vodka
½oz (15ml) dry vermouth

Chill the Martini glass thoroughly in the freezer or refrigerator for 2 or 4 hours respectively. Alternatively, fill the glass with ice.

Add a dash of yuzu juice or the yuzu zest to the mixing glass. Muddle (see page 33) the zest to release more essential oils from it.

Smack 3 shiso leaves between your palms to release their essential oils and drop into the mixing glass. Add the remaining ingredients. Fill the mixing glass with ice and stir for 30 seconds or until condensation forms on the outside. (Theoretically, you should be shaking, not stirring, as there is a dash of citrus in here, but you really don't want this cocktail to be cloudy, so we are breaking the rules.) If you used ice to chill your Martini glass, empty it out. Double-strain (see page 29) the cocktail into the chilled glass using the hawthorne strainer and tea strainer, to catch any particles of shiso or yuzu, and garnish with a whole shiso leaf.

SHISO AND YUZU MOJITO

Follow the directions for Hail the Kale (see page 196), but substitute shiso for mint and yuzu juice for lime juice.

The citrus fruit shiso is known for its anti-inflammatory properties and high levels of vitamins and minerals.

★

Yuzu juice or zest will provide an intense lime/grapefruit taste to your cocktails, but use in moderation. We use the zest in the Shiso Martini to keep the liquid as clear as possible. If you don't have fresh yuzu fruit, a dash of juice is fine.

Nasturtium COLLINS

Throughout summer and into the fall, nasturtiums grow out of control in the garden at Midnight Apothecary, so I feel no guilt about harvesting huge amounts to keep a semblance of order. They not only look glorious but they also taste wonderful. Both the leaves and flowers have a pepperiness that works particularly well with rum and tequila. We use Nasturtium Rum made with golden rum, not just for its flavor but also for the dramatic amber color you get once it is diluted against the yellow, orange, and red flowers.

1½oz (45ml) **Nasturtium Rum (see page 55)**

1oz (30ml) **Ginger Syrup (see page 70)**

½oz (15ml) **freshly squeezed lemon juice**

4oz (120ml) **soda water**

Tools: **Cocktail shaker with strainer**

Glass: **Collins**

Ice: **Cubes**

Garnish: **Nasturtium flowers, nasturtium leaves**

Serves 1

Fill the glass with ice. Pour the Nasturtium Rum, Ginger Syrup, and lemon juice into the cocktail shaker. Fill it two-thirds of the way up with ice, cover, and shake hard for 20 seconds. Strain the mixture into the glass over the ice. Top with the soda water, and garnish with the nasturtium flowers and leaves.

Nibble on the garnish of nasturtium leaves for an extra peppery kick.

Lemon Balm and
NASTURTIUM DAISY

Maybe there are a confusing number of flowers in this recipe name, but "daisy" refers purely to the style of cocktail. A Daisy is really an oversized Sour, which is liquor, citrus, and sugar, with extra ice, usually a fruit-based syrup, and a dash of soda water. Accounts of Daisies and what constitutes one have differed for over 100 years, so I am taking the usual liberties. Here I have once again included nasturtiums, because I can't get enough of them, but this time the base is Nasturtium Gin, to which I've added a small amount of Lemon Balm Liqueur and a slug of Sloe Blossom Syrup. Store-bought orgeat syrup will work just as well for that almond flavor.

2oz (60ml) Nasturtium Gin (see page 55)

2 tsp (10ml) Lemon Balm Liqueur (see page 65)

½oz (15ml) Sloe Blossom Syrup (see page 93) or orgeat syrup

½oz (15ml) freshly squeezed lemon juice

Dash of soda water

Tools: **Cocktail shaker with strainer**
Glass: **Rocks**
Ice: **Cracked**
Garnish: **Lemon zest, lemon balm (*Melissa officinalis*) leaf, nasturtium leaf**

Serves 1

Fill the glass with ice. Combine all the ingredients, except the soda water and garnish, in the cocktail shaker. Fill it two-thirds of the way up with ice. Cover and shake hard for 20 seconds. Strain the mixture into the glass over the ice. Add the garnish, and top with a dash of soda water.

Pumpkin and Carrot LOVE-IN

This is an autumnal/winter cocktail that we often serve around Halloween and Bonfire Night at Midnight Apothecary. As well as growing our own pumpkins for carving jack-o'-lanterns, we now also have a few small, sweet, denser sugar/baking pumpkins for making our own Roasted Pumpkin and Carrot Juice Purée for this cocktail. The sweet, earthy smokiness of the purée and Charred Sage Syrup are balanced in this cocktail by small amounts of citrus. If you like, use maple syrup in place of the Charred Sage Syrup. It's all topped off with ginger beer to give a bit of a hot kick and help fend off the cold night air.

Instead of making Roasted Pumpkin and Carrot Juice Purée, you can buy cans of pumpkin purée and add a dash of carrot juice to get the right consistency. However, the aroma and taste are so much greater when you make your own.

1½oz (45ml) dark, spiced rum

1½ tbsp (45ml) Roasted Pumpkin and Carrot Juice Purée (see below)

1 tbsp (15ml) Charred Sage Syrup (see page 78) or maple syrup

1 tsp (5ml) freshly squeezed lemon juice

2 tsp (10ml) freshly squeezed orange juice

Dash of orange bitters

Approximately 2oz (60ml) ginger beer (adjust to taste)

Tools: **Cocktail shaker with strainer**
Glass: **Collins**
Ice: **Cubes**
Garnish: **Baby carrot, with top**

Serves 1

Fill the glass with ice and add the baby carrot, with a few tops still attached, if possible. Add the rum, Roasted Pumpkin and Carrot Juice Purée, Charred Sage Syrup or maple syrup, lemon and orange juice, and dash of orange bitters to the cocktail shaker. Fill it two-thirds of the way up with ice. Cover and shake hard for 20 seconds. Strain the mixture into the glass over the ice. Top with ginger beer, according to taste, and garnish with a baby carrot.

ROASTED PUMPKIN AND CARROT JUICE PURÉE

This recipe makes approximately 1 cup (250ml) or five servings.

1 small pumpkin
¼ cup (50ml) carrot juice

Sharp knife
Spoon
Roasting pan
Parchment paper
Cooling tray and plate
Blender
Fine sieve
Measuring pitcher
Flexible scraper

Preheat the oven to 400°F (205°C). Wash and halve the pumpkin. Scoop out the seeds and pulp, reserving the seeds, if desired, to toast for an optional garnish. Slice the pumpkin into wedges and place face down on a roasting pan lined with parchment paper. Cook for 1–1 ½ hours. You will know when it is ready when the flesh is very tender.

Place the pumpkin wedges on a cooling tray with a plate underneath to catch the water that will drip from them. Let the pumpkin cool, then squeeze out the excess water. Scoop out the flesh and place in a blender. Purée for about a minute until the mix is smooth. Finally, pass the purée through the sieve into the measuring pitcher, using a flexible scraper to push all the mix through the fine holes.

Add ¼ cup (50ml) carrot juice to ¾ cup (150ml) pumpkin purée. Return to the blender to purée. This will store in the refrigerator in a sealed container for a couple of days.

Fennel, Tarragon, and Chard
COLLINS

This cocktail reeks of purity and piety but it's actually very refreshing. I wanted it to be clear, so I didn't juice the chard—if I had, the drink would have been a wonderful bright green. There's nothing wrong with that but I wanted to show off the delicate fennel (*Foeniculum vulgare*) fronds in the glass and the bright yellow of the rainbow chard (*Beta vulgaris* subsp. *cicla* var *flavescens*), which grows in a variety of colors, as you would expect from its name! Orange and fennel go wonderfully together, so I used the orange, lemon, and bergamot Oleo Saccharum, infused with French tarragon (*Artemisia dracunculus sativa*) and scented geranium. The Fennel-infused Gin and Elderflower Liqueur is a clear-ish spirit, so does a good job in taste as well as appearance.

1½oz (45ml) **Fennel-infused Gin** (see page 53)

½oz (15ml) **Elderflower Liqueur** (see page 57)

½oz (15ml) **Oleo Saccharum** (see page 108) or **Simple Syrup** (see page 68)

Approximately ¼oz (7ml) **freshly squeezed lemon juice** (adjust to taste)

Approximately 4oz (120ml) **soda water** (adjust to taste)

Tools: **Mixing glass, barspoon/long spoon, strainer**

Glass: **Collins**

Ice: **Cubes**

Garnish: **Fennel fronds, rainbow chard leaf, fennel flower, tender rainbow chard shoot**

Serves 1

Fill the Collins glass with ice. Wedge the garnish of fennel fronds between the ice cubes and the glass. Add the Fennel-infused Gin, Elderflower Liqueur, Oleo Saccharum or Simple Syrup, and lemon juice to the mixing glass. Fill with ice and stir for about 20 seconds until condensation appears on the outside. Strain the mixture into the Collins glass over the ice. Top with soda water and garnish with the rainbow chard leaf, fennel flower, and tender rainbow chard shoot, for nibbling on.

> This cocktail is a composite of the sight and scent I experienced as I brushed past our bed of young rainbow chard and fennel at different stages of growth.

BLOODY *Rosemary*

I included two "Bloody Rosemary" cocktails in this book: this garden cocktail and a "wild" variation (see page 165). The reason why there are two is that the combination of blood oranges, which appear in early spring, and rosemary, which starts to flower at the same time, is irresistible. This version is an indulgent, colorful drink. It's still on the sweet side, but the herbal notes of the rosemary in the essential oils, released by smacking a fresh sprig between your palms, as well as adding a small amount of rosemary simple syrup, together with the bitter notes of the peach bitters, redeem it. Bitter and sweet—that's love.

1 blood orange wheel

1 rosemary sprig

1oz (30ml) floral gin, such as Jensen Old Tom

1oz (30ml) blood orange liqueur, such as Solerno

2 tsp (10ml) Rosemary Syrup (see page 80)

½oz (15ml) freshly squeezed lemon juice

½oz (15ml) freshly squeezed blood orange juice

3 dashes of peach bitters

Tools: **Cocktail shaker with strainer, tea strainer**

Glass: **Rocks**

Ice: **Cubes**

Garnish: **Flowering rosemary sprig**

Serves 1

Place the blood orange wheel inside the glass. Smack the rosemary sprig between your palms to release the essential oils and place in the cocktail shaker. Add the remaining ingredients, and fill the shaker two-thirds of the way up with ice. Cover and shake hard for 20 seconds. Fill the glass with ice. Double-strain the cocktail (see page 29) into the glass, using the tea strainer to catch the rosemary needles. Garnish with the flowering rosemary sprig.

> **The blood orange liqueur Solerno provides the most fantastic red color that you would expect from blood oranges.**

VERY RUM *and Berry*

This recipe is a good chance to use any fruity purées you have going spare. Dark rum is punchy enough to take on quite strong, fruity flavors, so you can take your pick. You will need to add some sweetener in the form of Simple Syrup but if you have a flavored syrup, such as Chocolate Mint Syrup, to hand, this would add a refreshing and complementary note to the cocktail. Test and adjust for sweetness in any case because different fruits provide their own levels in the purée, but that won't be enough to balance the sweetness of the whole cocktail.

1 mint sprig

2oz (60ml) dark rum

1oz (30ml) Summer Berry Purée (see page 128)

½oz (15ml) Chocolate Mint Syrup (see page 80) or Simple Syrup (see page 68)

¾oz (22ml) freshly squeezed lemon juice

Soda water

Tools: **Cocktail shaker with strainer**

Glass: **Collins**

Ice: **Cubes**

Garnish: **Whole raspberries/other berries, mint sprig**

Serves 1

Fill the glass with ice. Smack the sprig of mint between your palms to release the essential oils and drop into the cocktail shaker. Add all the other ingredients (except the soda water), cover, and shake hard for 20 seconds. Strain the mixture and pour into the glass over the ice. Garnish with raspberries and a sprig of mint. Add a splash of soda water and serve.

FORAGED COCKTAILS

I'm not going to pretend that you can create an orgy of the senses with a few twigs and a couple of wild flowers. But when carefully considered wild ingredients are combined with good-quality liquor, you will enjoy some mouthwatering and unusual cocktails. My favorite has to be the Woodland Martini (page 170) for its ability to take me back to the sights and smells of a walk in a pine forest. It's also hard to beat a Gorse Collins (page 161) on a coastal picnic surrounded by the gorse blossoms themselves. Matching the right liquor to the foraged ingredient is half the fun; the other half is the adventure you had in the first place to get the ingredients.

If all else fails, you can substitute the wild ingredients with store-bought or garden-grown ingredients. This is not a "survivalist" handbook—and no points are deducted for "cheating!"

Blackberry MARTINI

Blackberrying with my mother when I was a young child formed my love of foraging and adventures with free food. The pleasure of finding those big, scented, sun-warmed berries, with their juice that drips down your fingers and chin, is hard to beat. You can add a sprig of mint to this recipe, but I prefer just a touch of blackcurrant cassis or blackberry liqueur instead, which gives that added indulgence.

2oz (60ml) floral gin, such as Jensen Old Tom

1oz (30ml) Blackberry Purée (see page 128)

2 tsp (10ml) Grand Marnier

2 tsp (10ml) blackcurrant cassis or blackberry liqueur

2 tsp (10ml) freshly squeezed lemon juice

Tools: **Blender, cocktail shaker with strainer**

Glass: **Martini**

Ice: **Cubes**

Garnish: **Blackberry and mint leaf on a toothpick (cocktail stick)**

Serves 1

Chill the glass thoroughly in the freezer or refrigerator for 2 or 4 hours respectively. Alternatively, fill the glass with ice.

Pour all the ingredients into the cocktail shaker, fill it two-thirds of the way up with ice, cover, and shake hard for 20 seconds. If you used ice to chill your Martini glass, empty it out. Strain the contents of the shaker into the chilled glass. Pierce the blackberry and mint sprig with the toothpick (cocktail stick) and serve.

You may need to adjust the level of sweetness based on the sugar levels of the blackberries you pick. Add an additional dash of cassis or Simple Syrup (see page 68) until the taste is just right.

THE MIGHTY *Meadowsweet*

Meadowsweet (*Filipendula ulmaria*) is ridiculously delicious in a syrup, and its almond and honey notes come to the fore in this cocktail. The blossom appears at the height of summer, so this tastes of summer nights to me. The oranges in the Grand Marnier and the sweet, nutty, spicy, vanilla, and floral notes of an oak-barrel-aged brandy as fine as cognac are a perfect marriage with the meadowsweet.

1½oz (45ml) cognac
2 tsp (10ml) Grand Marnier
½oz (15ml) Meadowsweet Syrup (see page 86)
¾oz (22ml) freshly squeezed lemon juice
Dash of orange bitters

Tools: **Cocktail shaker with strainer**
Glass: **Martini**
Ice: **Cubes**
Garnish: **Small sprig of meadowsweet blossom**

Serves 1

Chill the glass thoroughly in the freezer or refrigerator for 2 or 4 hours respectively. Alternatively, fill the glass with ice.

Pour all the ingredients into the cocktail shaker. Fill the shaker two-thirds of the way up with ice. Cover and shake hard for 20 seconds. If you used ice to chill your glass, empty it out. Strain the contents of the shaker into the chilled glass. Garnish with a small section of (bug-free) meadowsweet blossom.

You can skimp on the quality of the brandy if you wish, but if you have the opportunity to use a good cognac, you are not wasting it by diluting it. You are simply making a beautifully balanced cocktail.

Wild Plum SMASH

The cherry plums that are strained off in the Wild Cherry Plum Brandy recipe will work perfectly here, as the level of booze in them will give quite a kick. Both thyme and rosemary go well with plums, so use Rosemary or Thyme Syrup for sweetness, if you have any.

Tools: **Muddler**
Glass: **Rocks**
Ice: **Crushed (see page 32)**
Garnish: **Lemon wedge, sprig of rosemary/thyme**

Serves 1

3 brandy-soaked wild cherry plums (left over from making Wild Cherry Plum Brandy, see page 66)

¼oz (7ml) Rosemary or Thyme Syrup (see page 80) or Simple Syrup (see page 68)

Sprig of rosemary or thyme (optional)

½ lemon, cut into 3 wedges (reserve 1 wedge for garnish)

1½oz (45ml) Wild Cherry Plum Brandy (see page 66)

Remove the pit (stone) from the plums and add to the base of the glass with the Rosemary, Thyme, or Simple Syrup. If you have used plain simple syrup, add a sprig of rosemary or thyme. Gently muddle the plums and syrup, then add 2 lemon wedges, and muddle those as well to really release the juice. Add crushed ice three-quarters of the way up the glass. Pour the Wild Cherry Plum Brandy over the ice. Garnish with a lemon wedge and fresh sprig of rosemary or thyme.

SLOE Time

This is one of those cozy winter cocktails. Sloe gin is a winner but adding rhubarb and ginger compote gives it body, while the apple and rhubarb juice and freshly squeezed lemon juice cut through the sweetness. So yes, it's a Sour, but I prefer this name.

2oz (60ml) Sloe Gin (see page 62)

2 tsp rhubarb and ginger compote from Rhubarb and Ginger Syrup (see page 79)

1oz (30ml) apple and rhubarb juice

¾oz (22ml) freshly squeezed lemon juice

Tools: **Cocktail shaker, hawthorne strainer, tea strainer**
Glass: **Martini**
Ice: **Cubes**
Garnish: **Shard of freshly peeled ginger**

Serves 1

Chill the glass thoroughly in the freezer or refrigerator for 2 or 4 hours respectively. Alternatively, fill the glass with ice.

Pour all the ingredients into the cocktail shaker and fill it two-thirds of the way up with ice. Cover and shake hard for 20 seconds to really incorporate the compote. If you used ice to chill the glass, empty it out. Double-strain (see page 29) the contents of the shaker into the chilled glass, using a hawthorne strainer and a tea strainer to catch the tiny pieces of compote. Garnish with a shard of fresh ginger.

Hedgerow SOUR

The color and texture, let alone exquisite taste, of this winter cocktail is a worthy prize for your foraging efforts. Rosehips, around from late summer into the winter, provide exotic floral elegance. Crab apples, while impossibly sour uncooked, are transformed into a thick, pectin-rich, orangey-pink, appley, almost tropical syrup. The pressed juice of the raw crab apples in the Crab Apple Verjuice provides us with malic acid to balance the sweetness. The egg white tones down the strength and also the sweetness, and creates a delicious mouth-feel.

2oz (6oml) floral gin, such as Jensen Old Tom

¾oz (22ml) Crab Apple Verjuice (see page 107) or freshly squeezed lemon juice

½oz (15ml) Crab Apple Syrup (see page 90)

½oz (15ml) Rosehip Syrup (see page 89)

1 egg white

Tools: **Cocktail shaker with strainer**

Glass: **Martini**

Ice: **Cubes**

Garnish: **Candied rosehip, lemon spiral (see page 35), toothpick (cocktail stick)**

Serves 1

Chill the glass thoroughly in the freezer or refrigerator for 2 or 4 hours respectively. Alternatively, fill the glass with ice.

Add all the ingredients to the cocktail shaker, cover, and dry-shake hard (see page 33) for 30 seconds. Fill the shaker two-thirds of the way up with ice, cover again, and shake hard again for 20 seconds. If you used ice to chill your glass, empty it out. Strain the contents of the shaker into the chilled glass. Skewer the candied rosehip onto the toothpick (cocktail stick) and wrap the lemon spiral around it. Serve immediately.

> Rosehips are packed with vitamin C to fend off winter colds, and it is claimed that the pectin found in apples may help reduce cholesterol, so we're taking care of you here!

Wild Strawberry and Rose
DAIQUIRI

Strawberries and roses are from the same family (Rosaceae) that gives us so much pleasure, from apples and pears to these two beauties. Wild strawberries (*Fragraria vesca* or *F. virginiana*) are those tiny, jewel-like treasures that you sometimes find in woodland clearings and meadows, on forest edges and along trails, and even in some quiet urban areas. Here they are combined with white rum and Rose Petal Syrup, together with crushed ice, to conjure up summer meadows on a hot day.

People have been gorging on wild strawberries since the Stone Age, and for good reason. They are much sweeter than their commercial cousins and, when sold in stores, are considered a very expensive delicacy.

The wild strawberry, which produces white flowers before the familiar red berries arrive, is a creeping perennial that spreads along the ground by runners that form new roots and plants. Try growing some in a shady spot to get your own precious bounty.

1½oz (45ml) white rum
¾oz (22ml) Rose Petal Syrup (see page 75)
2 tsp (10ml) freshly squeezed lime juice
10 wild strawberries or 3 large strawberries, hulled and halved
⅔ cup (100g) crushed ice (see page 32)

Tools: **Blender**
Glass: **Rocks**
Garnish: **3 wild strawberries, toothpick (cocktail stick)**

Serves 1

Combine all the ingredients in the blender and pulse/blend at a high speed for 30 seconds or until smooth. Pour into the glass. Garnish with 3 wild strawberries on a toothpick (cocktail) stick.

Wild Violet SOUR

This delicious spring cocktail should provide an extraordinary color. However, your Wild Violet Syrup may be quite pale and, in any case, it will turn pink when combined with lemon, so I suggest you add a couple of dashes of cassis to intensify the violet shade. If you do, add a couple more drops of lemon juice.

Tools: Cocktail shaker with strainer

Glass: Martini

Ice: Cubes

Garnish: Wild violet flower/candied wild violet flower (see page 34)

Serves 1

1½oz (45ml) dry gin

¾oz (22ml) Wild Violet Syrup (see page 71)

½oz (15ml) freshly squeezed lemon juice

1 dash of crème de cassis or other blackcurrant/blackberry liqueur (optional)

1 egg white

Chill the glass thoroughly in the freezer or refrigerator for 2 or 4 hours respectively. Alternatively, fill the glass with ice.

Pour all the ingredients into the cocktail shaker. Cover and dry-shake hard for 20 seconds (see page 33) to emulsify the egg white. Fill the shaker two-thirds of the way up with ice, cover, and shake hard for another 20 seconds. If you used ice to chill the glass, empty it out. Strain the contents of the shaker into the chilled glass. Garnish with a fresh or candied wild violet flower.

Gorse COLLINS

When I experiment with cocktails, I usually start with the flavor that I want to bring to the fore and work from there. Gorse Flower Syrup has a beautiful but delicate almond and honey flavor, which I didn't want to overpower, but it does need a spirit with a complementary flavor, rather than a tasteless vodka, say, or the drink will be insipid. I decided that our False Acacia Gin would be perfect. The honey overtones in both the gin and the gorse syrup work really well and there is no cloying sweetness. Gorse (*Ulex europaeus*) and juniper grow in similar conditions and seem very happy together combined in a cocktail. If you don't have any False Acacia Gin, experiment with a good-quality gin with plenty of juniper coming through.

1½oz (45ml) False Acacia Gin (see page 51)

1oz (30ml) Gorse Flower Syrup (see page 76)

½oz (15ml) freshly squeezed lemon juice

Approximately 3oz (90ml) soda water (according to taste)

Tools: **Cocktail shaker with strainer**
Glass: **Collins**
Ice: **Cubes**
Garnish: **Individual gorse blossoms**

Serves 1

Fill the glass with ice. Pour the False Acacia Gin, Gorse Flower Syrup, and lemon juice into the cocktail shaker. Fill two-thirds of the way up with ice. Cover, shake hard for 20 seconds, then strain the contents into the glass over the ice. Garnish with individual gorse blossoms and top with soda water.

Wild Cherry MANHATTAN

This is such a classic drink that I don't want to go too far off-piste with my recipe. The type of cherries used in your Wild Cherry-infused Rye Whiskey are going to affect the sweetness but whether they are sour or sweet cherries, this drink will work beautifully. The bitters will offset the fruity, sweeter notes in the Carpano Antica vermouth and any sweeter cherries in the rye. With just the right balance of bitter, sweet, and smooth, it is certainly worth the extra expense.

2oz (60ml) Wild Cherry-infused Rye Whiskey (see page 45)

1oz (30ml) Carpano Antica vermouth

3 dashes of Wild Cherry Bitters (see pages 102–103) or chocolate bitters

Tools: **Mixing glass, stirring rod/long spoon, julep strainer/hawthorne strainer**

Glass: **Martini/rocks**

Ice: **Cubes (optional), cracked (see page 32)**

Garnish: **Orange twist (see page 35), pair of chocolate-dipped cherries (optional)**

Serves 1

Chill the Martini glass thoroughly in the freezer or refrigerator for 2 or 4 hours respectively. Alternatively, fill the glass with ice.

Pour the Wild Cherry-infused Rye Whiskey, vermouth, and bitters into the mixing glass. Fill it two-thirds of the way up with cracked ice. Stir for at least 30 seconds (or a minimum of 50 revolutions) until there is condensation on the outside.

If you used ice to chill your Martini glass, empty it out. Slide the julep strainer inside, or the hawthorne strainer over, the mixing glass and strain the contents into the Martini glass. Garnish with an orange twist—and for an extra treat, a pair of chocolate-dipped cherries.

The key to making the perfect Manhattan is in the mixing. You need to stir, not shake, because it needs to be clear, and you also need cracked ice (see page 32) to ensure the maximum surface area of ice comes into contact with the liquid—on no account use crushed ice, as that will overdilute the drink.

You can make this cocktail with cherry-infused bourbon instead of rye—it will just be a little sweeter.

For an alternative garnish, add a rye-soaked fresh cherry or a rye-soaked and chocolate-dipped cherry, if you are so inclined, for that added element of kitsch.

APPLE *Crisp*

The herbal, resinous flavor of rosemary lifts this cocktail into autumnal wonderland. Rowan Syrup imparts a floral, almost bitter/sweet/acid appley taste—until you've tried it, you won't believe it's possible to get all those tastes from one syrup, but it's true. And it's a beautiful orange-red color. An aged Reposado tequila provides a punchy, earthy, sweet smokiness. I forage for eating apples to make the apple juice—simply juice them—and for crab apples to make the Crab Apple Verjuice, which provides the acidity. You could, of course, use lemon juice instead.

1 rosemary sprig
½oz (15ml) Rowan Syrup (see page 92)
1oz (30ml) cider brandy
1oz (30ml) Reposado tequila
¾oz (22ml) Crab Apple Verjuice (see page 107) or ½oz (15ml) freshly squeezed lemon juice
¾oz (22ml) apple juice

Tools: **Cocktail shaker with strainer, tea strainer**
Glass: **Wine/rocks**
Ice: **Cubes**
Garnish: **Apple slices made into a fan (see page 34), rosemary sprig**

Serves 1

Smack the rosemary sprig hard in the palm of your hands to release the essential oils and drop into the cocktail shaker. Add the remaining ingredients. Fill the shaker two-thirds of the way up with ice. Cover and shake hard for 20 seconds. Double-strain (see page 29) the contents of the shaker into the glass, using the tea strainer to catch the rosemary needles. Garnish with an apple fan and a rosemary sprig.

I use a Somerset apple brandy because we want to support small U.K. suppliers but calvados, applejack, or cider brandy from a small batch distillery will do the job just as well.

I serve this cocktail over ice in a big wine glass in the summer, but straight up in a rocks glass in the winter.

WILD BLOODY *Rosemary*

This cocktail is meant to be a post-dinner fireside warmer for a hot date—and blood oranges are apt for matters of the heart. Orange, cherries, and rosemary make an excellent sweet/savory/aromatic combination. Rosemary has traditionally been offered over the centuries as a symbol of love, loyalty, and fidelity. And cherries... well, I'll leave you to make your own analogy.

2 tsp (10ml) Blood Orange, Grapefruit, and Rosemary Oleo Saccharum (see page 108)

3 dashes of Wild Cherry Bitters (see pages 102–103) or angostura bitters

2oz (60ml) Wild Cherry Plum Brandy (see page 66)

½oz (15ml) blood orange liqueur, such as Solerno

Splash of soda water

Tools: **Barspoon/wooden spoon**

Glass: **Rocks**

Ice: **Cubes**

Garnish: **Rosemary sprig (flowering if possible), blood orange wheel**

Serves 1

Pour the Oleo Saccharum into the bottom of the glass. Add the Wild Cherry Bitters. Use the barspoon or the end of a wooden spoon to combine the syrup and bitters, and line the whole of the bottom of the glass. Fill the glass with ice. Pour over the Wild Cherry Plum Brandy and blood orange liqueur. Stir to mix and chill the drink. Place the blood orange wheel vertically on the inside edge of the glass. Garnish with a flowering rosemary sprig. Add the merest splash of soda water. Serve immediately.

> This is, in essence, a traditional Old Fashioned, although purists would baulk at the addition of a splash of blood orange liqueur, the amount of oily sugar in the form of Oleo Saccharum (see page 108), and replacing the angostura bitters. So, I've given it another name altogether.

The CHERRY BLOSSOM

Japan is known for its cherry blossom celebrations—a very short season when this beautiful flower takes center stage—and even on London streets, the drama of cherry blossoms (*Prunus serrulata*) falling from the trees like confetti is not just a visual feast. The blossoms themselves can be candied for a wonderful garnish (see page 34) or dried and mixed with salt for a cocktail rim (see page 35). I have used Japanese ingredients in this cocktail to bring a little of Japan to London.

¾oz (22ml) yuzu or lemon juice
Dried pink cherry blossom, ground into pink salt (see page 35)
1oz (30ml) plum wine
1oz (30ml) vodka
½oz (15ml) sake
2 tsp (10ml) sour cherry juice

Tools: **Saucer, cocktail shaker with strainer**
Glass: **Martini**
Ice: **Cubes**
Garnish: **Candied pink cherry blossom (see page 34)**

Serves 1

Chill the glass thoroughly in the freezer or refrigerator for 2 or 4 hours respectively.

Dip the glass into a saucer of yuzu or lemon juice and then turn the outside edge of the glass into the salted cherry blossom mix. Pour the remaining ingredients into the cocktail shaker, fill it two-thirds of the way up with ice, and shake hard for 20 seconds. Strain the contents of the shaker into the chilled glass and garnish with a candied pink cherry blossom.

> **The yuzu fruit is commonly used in Japan as a lemon substitute, with its overtones of grapefruit and mandarin. You can order it online from Japanese suppliers.**

The Elder SOUR

The Elder Sour is a well-known cocktail—some people use vodka, others gin, and some just Elderflower Liqueur, which, in this case, is vodka-based. This is a pure celebration of the elderflower so we are keeping it simple, with lemon and lime juices providing the right balance of acidity to cut through the liqueur.

**2oz (60ml) Elderflower Liqueur
(see page 57)**
**½oz (15ml) freshly squeezed
lime juice**
**½oz (15ml) freshly squeezed
lemon juice**
1 egg white
Dash of orange bitters

Tools: **Cocktail shaker with strainer**
Glass: **Martini**
Ice: **Cubes**
Garnish: **Elderflower blossom sprig**

Serves 1

Chill the glass thoroughly in the freezer or refrigerator for 2 or 4 hours respectively. Alternatively, fill the glass with ice.

Add all the ingredients to the cocktail shaker, cover, and dry-shake hard for at least 20 seconds (see page 33), to emulsify the egg. Fill the shaker two-thirds of the way up with ice, cover, and shake hard for another 20 seconds. If you used ice to chill the glass, empty it out. Strain the contents of the shaker into the chilled glass. Garnish with a sprig of elderflower blossom.

ELDERBERRY *Me*

Elderberries are mildly toxic when eaten raw in quantity, so only use a very few on a sprig for the garnish. The goodness of the elderberries will be outweighed by the hefty amount of cream you are consuming. This cocktail is delicious!

1½oz (45ml) coffee liqueur, such as Tia Maria or Kahlua

¾oz (22ml) heavy (double) cream

½oz (15ml) Elderberry and Clove Syrup (see page 88)

¾oz (22ml) freshly squeezed lemon juice

Dash of soda water (according to taste)

Fill the glass with ice. Pour all the ingredients (except the soda water) into the cocktail shaker, cover, and shake hard for 20 seconds to fully incorporate the cream. Strain the contents of the shaker into the glass over the ice. Top with a dash of soda water (adjust to taste). Garnish with a sprig of elderberries.

Tools: **Cocktail shaker with strainer**

Glass: **Collins**

Ice: **Cubes**

Garnish: **Vey small elderberry sprig**

Serves 1

Woodland MARTINI

The idea of this cocktail is for it to taste and smell like a walk in the woods. The clean, lemony pine scent and flavor of the Douglas Fir Vodka shines through, accompanied by just a hint of smoky sweetness from the Charred Sage Syrup. The vermouth and lemon juice balance out all the flavors to leave the cocktail on the dry side.

2oz (60ml) Douglas Fir Vodka (see page 53)

½oz (15ml) Charred Sage Syrup (see page 78)

½oz (15ml) Wild Vermouth (see pages 98–99)

2 tsp (10ml) freshly squeezed lemon juice

Tools: **Cocktail shaker with strainer**

Glass: **Martini**

Ice: **Cubes**

Garnish: **Young Douglas Fir** (*Pseudotsuga menziesii*) **tip**

Serves 1

Pour all the ingredients into the cocktail shaker and fill it two-thirds \of the way up with ice. Cover and shake hard for 20 seconds. Strain the contents of the shaker into the glass. Garnish with a young Douglas Fir tip.

BERRIED *Treasure*

This is essentially a French 77 cocktail, which uses Elderflower Liqueur to provide the sweetness, unlike the French 75, which uses simple syrup, in addition to gin, lemon juice, and champagne. I have no idea why it is called a French 77 when you use elderflower liqueur!

This take on the French 75/77 garnish (see box) uses berry flavor pearls, available from online gourmet catering suppliers. These "bullets" of flavor are made from foraged fruit like blackberries, rose hips, crab apples, and sloes. I would recommend serving this drink with a long spoon, so that your guests can savor the tiny jewels in its hidden depths.

1 tsp berry flavor pearls

2oz (60ml) gin

½oz (15ml) Elderflower Liqueur (see page 57)

1oz (30ml) freshly squeezed lemon juice

2oz (60ml) champagne, prosecco, or other dry sparkling wine

Tools: **Cocktail shaker with strainer**

Glass: **Champagne flute**

Ice: **Cubes**

Garnish: **Lemon spiral (see page 35), long teaspoon/barspoon**

Serves 1

Place the flavor pearls in the bottom of the champagne flute. Pour the gin, Elderflower Liqueur, and lemon juice into the cocktail shaker. Fill it two-thirds of the way up with ice. Cover and shake hard for 20 seconds. Strain the contents into the flute. Top up with champagne or sparkling wine. Garnish with a lemon spiral and serve with a long spoon.

> **In case you're interested in the origins of the names of drinks, the French 75 was created in 1915 in Paris and was said to "have such a kick that it felt like being shelled with the powerful French 75mm field gun." Bullets are sometimes placed in the bottom of the glass as a garnish.**

Prunus 'Shogetsu' COCKTAIL

This is a variation on a Japanese theme, using the beautiful white cherry blossom from the *Prunus* 'Shogetsu'.

1oz (30ml) plum wine
1oz (30ml) sake
1oz (30ml) vodka
1-in (2.5-cm) fresh ginger, peeled and thinly sliced

Tools: **Mixing glass, barspoon/long spoon, julep strainer, tea strainer**

Glass: **Wine**

Ice: **Cubes**

Garnish: ***Prunus* 'Shogetsu' blossom**

Serves 1

Combine all the ingredients in the mixing glass and fill it two-thirds of the way up with ice. Stir for 30 seconds or until condensation appears on the outside. Place the julep strainer inside the mixing glass and double-strain (see page 29) the contents into the wine glass, using a tea strainer to catch any pieces of ginger. Garnish with a white cherry blossom (*Prunus* 'Shogetsu').

The Ultimate BLOODY MARY

We call this The Firework at our annual Bonfire Night Spectaculars in November at Midnight Apothecary. If it doesn't blow the cobwebs away and warm you up, you're lost to us! The Horseradish and Black Cardamom Vodka provides the heat and the smoke. We don't serve this over ice because the ice cubes would water down the rich tomato juice and that would be unpleasant. We also don't want the tomato juice to get frothy from shaking, so we "roll" the cocktail, which allows us to cool down the drink without the said frothiness.

2oz (60ml) Horseradish and Black Cardamom Vodka (see page 44)

4oz (120ml) good-quality, thick tomato juice

2 tsp (10ml) freshly squeezed lemon juice

2 dashes of Tabasco

2 dashes of Worcestershire sauce

1 pinch of celery salt

1 tsp amontillado sherry

Tools: **Pitcher, barspoon/wooden spoon, 2 mixing glasses, cocktail shaker with strainer**

Glass: **Collins**

Ice: **Cubes**

Garnish: **Lovage/celery/fennel stalk, nasturtium leaves and flowers (if available)**

Serves 1

Add all the ingredients, except the sherry, to the pitcher and give them a stir with the barspoon or the end of the wooden spoon, so that you are ready to "roll" (see page 33). Swirl the sherry around the inside of the Collins glass to "rinse" it, coating as much of the surface as possible. Fill one of the mixing glasses two-thirds of the way up with ice. Pour the mix in the pitcher into this mixing glass and then immediately "roll," or transfer, the whole mix, including the ice, into the empty mixing glass. Repeat back and forth between the mixing glasses until your drink is cold. Pour into the cocktail shaker, then immediately strain the mix into the Collins glass. Garnish with a celery, lovage, or fennel stalk, and nasturtium leaves and flowers.

"Rinsing" the glass with amontillado sherry gives a hint of rich sweetness but nothing more.

If we have any young nasturtium leaves or flowers (unlikely in late fall, but occasionally they are around), we pop them in the glass as a garnish for color and some added pepperiness.

THE *Yarrow*

The bittersweet taste of the tequila has been balanced by adjusting the ratios of ingredients in a classic Sour to two parts strong, one part sour, and half part sweet, and adding three dashes of bitters. It makes for a very refreshing cocktail on the dry side.

2oz (60ml) Reposado tequila
½oz (15ml) Yarrow Syrup (see page 94)
1oz (30ml) freshly squeezed lemon juice
3 dashes of Wild Cherry Bitters (see pages 102–103)

Tools: **Cocktail shaker with strainer**
Glass: **Martini**
Ice: **Cubes**
Garnish: **Wild yarrow (*Achillea millefolium*) flower**

Serves 1

Chill the glass thoroughly in the freezer or refrigerator for 2 or 4 hours respectively. Alternatively, fill the glass with ice.

Add all the ingredients to the cocktail shaker. Fill it two-thirds of the way up with ice. Cover and shake hard for 10 seconds. If you used ice to chill your glass, empty it out. Strain the cocktail into the chilled glass, and garnish with a wild yarrow flower.

Yarrow is used extensively for its medicinal properties—from Greek hero Achilles who staunched the bleeding of his wounded soldiers with the herb to the Cherokee tribes who drank yarrow tea to reduce fever and aid sleep. A word of caution, though: pregnant women should not consume yarrow as it contains small quantities of thujone, which is a uterine stimulant.

Blackberry and Lilac
COBBLER

Blackberries and Lilac Syrup were put together for no other reason than they were sitting next to each other in the refrigerator and I decided to have a play. The Sloe Gin was a natural choice for the dark fruity blackberries. I've also been playing around with mezcal as its earthy smokiness fits the vibe of Midnight Apothecary metaphorically, although not always practically—it's a tricky ingredient to match. But in this case, it works with the lilac (*Syringa vulgaris*), blackberries, and Sloe Gin to provide a great little cocktail.

Tools: **Muddler, cocktail shaker with strainer**

Glass: **Rocks**

Ice: **Crushed**

Garnish: **Blackberry, 3 individual lilac blossoms, short straw**

6 blackberries (save 1 for the garnish)

1 tsp (5ml) blackcurrant cassis

1½oz (45ml) Sloe Gin (see page 62)

1oz (30ml) mezcal

½oz (15ml) freshly squeezed lemon juice

Serves 1   **½oz (15ml) Lilac Syrup (see page 82)**

Fill the glass with crushed ice to just below the rim. Muddle 5 blackberries with the cassis (see page 33) in the bottom of the cocktail shaker. Add the other ingredients, cover, and shake hard, without ice, for 20 seconds. Strain the contents of the shaker over the crushed ice into the glass. Add the garnish of blackberry and lilac blossoms. Serve with a short straw.

NOCINO *Nights*

Nocino, a sweet, green walnut, Italian-style liqueur, is traditionally drunk on its own as a post-meal digestif. You could use it to accompany brandy as a Sidecar—you'll get oak from the brandy, and walnuts from the liqueur, in a nice nutty combo. But here we use our "What-on-earth-goes-with-this infusion?"— the Wild Fennel, Fig, Grilled Bergamot, and Star Anise Rum—with Nocino, along with some of our Wild Vermouth. For the bitters, a most important ingredient, you can use either our Wild Cherry Bitters or, to keep an element of tradition, some angostura bitters.

2oz (60ml) Wild Fennel, Fig, Grilled Bergamot, and Star Anise Rum (see page 48)

¾oz (22ml) Nocino (see page 61) or sweet vermouth

¾oz (22ml) Wild Vermouth (see pages 98–99) or sweet vermouth

3 dashes of Wild Cherry Bitters (see pages 102–103) or angostura bitters

Tools: **Mixing glass, stirring rod/long spoon, julep strainer/hawthorne strainer**

Glass: **Martini/rocks**

Ice: **Cracked (see page 32)**

Garnish: **Fresh cherry or 2-in (5-cm) piece of orange peel**

Serves 1

Chill the glass thoroughly in the freezer or refrigerator for 2 or 4 hours respectively. Alternatively, fill the glass with ice.

Pour the Wild Fennel Rum, Nocino, Wild Vermouth, and Wild Cherry Bitters in the mixing glass. Fill it two-thirds of the way up with cracked ice. Stir for at least 30 seconds (or a minimum of 50 revolutions) until there is condensation on the outside. If you used ice to chill your cocktail glass, empty it out. Slide the julep strainer inside, or the hawthorne strainer over, the mixing glass and strain the cocktail into the chilled glass. Garnish with a cherry or slice of orange peel.

The key to making this cocktail is how you mix it: you need to stir, not shake, to keep it clear.

Use cracked ice to ensure the maximum surface area of ice comes into contact with the liquid. On no account use crushed ice, as that will over-dilute the drink.

The HONEYSUCKLE

The stunning honeysuckle (*Lonicera periclymenum*) blossoms appear in early summer and provide a heady scent around the garden at Midnight Apothecary, as well as in the neighboring parks, railroad sidings, and streets. I have used some vodka here to maintain the strength of the cocktail but not drown out the taste of honeysuckle. The rowan in the foam provides bitter and sour notes to counteract the sweetness of the honey and sourness of the lemon. And rowan works beautifully with brandy. The sweet, sharp mint opens up the palate to make the drink balanced and refreshing.

5 spearmint (*Mentha spicata*) leaves
1oz (30ml) cognac (or mid-range brandy)
½oz (15ml) vodka
¾oz (22ml) Honeysuckle Syrup (see page 72)
¾oz (22ml) freshly squeezed lemon juice
Rowan, Honey, and Lemon Foam (see page 37)

Tools: **Cocktail shaker with strainer**
Glass: **Martini**
Ice: **Cubes**
Garnish: **Honeysuckle blossom**

Serves 1

Chill the glass thoroughly in the freezer or refrigerator for 2 or 4 hours respectively. Alternatively, fill the glass with ice.

Smack the mint leaves between the palms of your hands to release the essential oils and drop them into the cocktail shaker. Add the cognac, vodka, honeysuckle syrup, and lemon juice. Fill the shaker two-thirds of the way up with ice, cover, and shake hard for 20 seconds. If you used ice to chill your glass, empty it out. Strain the cocktail into the chilled glass. Remove the whipper containing the Rowan, Honey, and Lemon Foam from the refrigerator, shake it a few times, and, holding it vertically, gently discharge the foam until it reaches the level of the rim of the glass. Wait a few seconds for the foam to settle. Garnish with the honeysuckle blossom and serve.

The blossom heads are the perfect size to fill a champagne coupe or Martini glass as a garnish on top of the egg white foam. Encourage your guests to try to suck the nectar out of the blossoms, although the bees will usually have got there first.

Rotherhithe NOOSE

This cocktail owes its rather gruesome name to a pub just along the River Thames from Midnight Apothecary (see box), and was inspired by a cocktail called the Hangman's Blood—a 1-pint (half-a-liter) mix of gin, brandy, port, whisky, rum, and stout, which sounds lethal. The presence of gin and brandy got me thinking about our Beech Leaf Noyau and what to do with it. I wanted to play around with beer cocktails and this combination seems to work—it's certainly a lot less lethal than the Hangman's Blood.

2oz (60ml) Beech Leaf Noyau (see page 100), chilled

3oz (90ml) stout or porter, chilled

2oz (60ml) champagne or dry sparkling wine, chilled

Tools: **Barspoon/long spoon**
Glass: **Champagne flute**

Serves 1

Pour the Beech Leaf Noyau and stout into the champagne flute, and top up with champagne. I could suggest a flexible plant stalk, tied into a hangman's noose, as a garnish, but I'm not morbid!

The Prospect of Whitby has a balcony at the back with a hangman's noose swinging over the river. This is a nod to one notorious customer dating back to the 1680s: Judge Jeffreys, known as the "Hanging Judge," who, according to legend, was always either drunk or in a rage. Eventually fate caught up with him and he was caught by the locals and ended up dying a miserable death in the Tower of London.

You don't need any ice or mixing for this—just make sure that all your ingredients are thoroughly chilled in the refrigerator beforehand.

EPINÉ AND FENNEL
Negroni

A Negroni should open up your palate with a perfect balance of sweet, bitter, and herbal. You may ask yourself why on earth fennel would work with a liqueur made from red wine and brandy, which is the alcoholic base of Epiné. Well, the sweet, herbal, anise flavor of fennel goes well with almonds, which is the flavor you get from the blackthorn leaves, and also with brandy. So, somehow they all come together in a happy Negroni.

If I didn't have any Wild Vermouth to hand, I would go with a dry vermouth to counter the sweetness of the Epiné.

This cocktail's other name is Le Brunel. Why? Midnight Apothecary is based at the Brunel Museum, in a roof garden on top of the glorious underground Grand Entrance Hall to the Thames Tunnel in Rotherhithe, which was completed by Marc Brunel in 1843. He was an engineer and the father of Isambard Kingdom Brunel, arguably the U.K.'s greatest engineer. Marc was French, as is Epiné... hence the link.

1oz (30ml) Epiné (see page 63)
1oz (30ml) Fennel-infused Gin (see page 53)
1oz (30ml) Wild Vermouth (see pages 98–99)

Tools: **Barspoon/wooden spoon**
Glass: **Rocks**
Ice: **Cubes**
Garnish: **Fennel fronds, orange slice**

Serves 1

This drink could not be simpler to build. Simply fill the glass with ice. Pour the 3 ingredients into the glass. Stir with the barspoon or the end of a wooden spoon for 30 seconds or 50 revolutions, until the drink is properly chilled. Garnish with some fennel fronds and an orange slice.

May BOWL

This very simple punch originated in Germany and is traditionally served on May Day, a public holiday. Sweet woodruff (*Galium odoratum*) is a creeping herb found in shady patches under trees in parks, woods, and other dark corners. Its leaves and flowers provide sweet, herbal, vanilla, and woodsy notes to the dry white wine and champagne. The leaves and flowers need to be picked the day before making the punch, to dry out slightly and give off a stronger scent, so making this punch is a two-stage process.

1½ cups (1 small bunch) fresh sweet woodruff

1 cup (250ml) water

4 tbsp (60g) superfine (caster) sugar

750ml bottle of dry white wine, such as a German Riesling

750ml bottle of champagne or dry sparkling wine

Tools: **Baking sheet, sealable Tupperware box, paper towel, small nonreactive pan, wooden spoon, punch bowl, plastic wrap, ladle**

Glass: **Wine**

Ice: **Cubes or large sphere**

Garnish: **Fresh sweet woodruff leaf and/or flower**

Makes about 14 servings

Remove any damaged leaves from the bunch of sweet woodruff. Spread out about one-third of it on a baking sheet and place on the bottom shelf of a recently switched-off oven, with the door open, or in an airing cupboard, to dry out slightly overnight. Meanwhile, line a Tupperware box with a damp sheet of paper towel and place the remaining leaves and flowers inside to stay fresh. Seal the box and place in the refrigerator until just before you serve the punch.

About 2 hours before serving the punch, heat the water and sugar in the nonreactive pan, stirring until the sugar has dissolved. Let cool. Meanwhile, place the semi-dried woodruff in a punch bowl and pour the dry white wine over it. Cover with plastic wrap and place in the refrigerator for at least an hour.

As soon as the sugar syrup has cooled, add it to the punch bowl, stir, and return to the refrigerator for an hour. Before serving, remove the semi-dried woodruff with a ladle and replace with the fresh leaves and flowers from the Tupperware box. Serve in a wine glass topped up with champagne and garnished with a woodruff leaf and/or flower.

Drink this punch in moderation as sweet woodruff contains coumarin, which is toxic in large doses. If you stick to the amounts here, you'll be fine.

★

Sweet woodruff has been used since the Middle Ages to treat everything, from cuts to liver problems, and also to scent linens. Today, herbalists use this fantastic herb as an anti-inflammatory and to treat stomachache.

★

Strawberries, or even better, wild strawberries, would make a great addition to this punch, as would wild violet flowers and lemon slices. I, however, prefer the clean simplicity of sweet woodruff on its own.

MOCKTAILS *and* *Restorative* COCKTAILS

The plants we put in our drinks are fresh and therefore bursting with nutrients as well as flavor. Obviously sugar and alcohol in excess are not going to do you any favors, but using alcohol to extract the goodness from plants, as I do when making infusions, is no bad thing. Alcohol was, and still can be, the easiest way of dissolving their medical constituents and dispersing them into the body. After all, it's what apothecaries were doing by the mid-sixteenth century in today's equivalent role of community pharmacist. They understood that high-proof alcohol (80 proof/40% ABV or above) not only extracts useful volatile essences, but also opens the blood vessels and stimulates the heart, so that they are released into the body more quickly. And, if that isn't impressive enough, high-proof alcohol preserves those herbal extracts almost indefinitely.

Herb gardens developed in part to make medicines. For centuries, if not millennia, "wise women" and "healers" have understood the use of a huge variety of herbs for medicinal purposes. But, as much as alcohol can be a beneficial (and fun) way to take on these nutrients, there are plenty of delicious and healthy nonalcoholic "mocktails" to try. By using ingredients from your "garden cocktail cabinet," local market, or foraging plot, booze-free drinks do not have to be the boring alternative at a party, either in taste or appearance.

While most of the cocktails in this book offer at least some herbal goodness, those listed here are either nonalcoholic or particularly restorative, but you don't need to be pregnant or the designated driver before you try them. Treat yourself!

Red Clover LEMONADE

The beautiful flowers of red clover (*Trifolium pratense*) are slightly sweet, and many of us will have enjoyed them in clover honey. They are also packed with nutrients, calcium, magnesium, potassium, and vitamin C. Red clover has been used in tea form for many years to alleviate the symptoms of gout. This lemonade is a quick and easy recipe that leaves you with a very pretty, delicately flavored sweet drink—think sweet hay.

Coumarin, the slightly vanilla-flavored phytochemical present in red clover, has antifungal and antitumor properties, but it also thins the blood. While that may be great for some, people taking anticoagulants should not consume red clover in large quantities.

Many menopausal women who experience hot flashes (flushes) take red clover in some form because it is considered to be one of the highest sources of isoflavones, which act like estrogens.

3 cups (750ml) water
Approximately 40 red clover blossoms
1 cup (250ml) freshly squeezed lemon juice
3 tbsp (50ml) honey, preferably raw, set or runny
Soda water

Tools: **Small nonreactive pan, fine-strainer (see page 26), wide-mouthed pitcher, wooden spoon,**
Glass: **Collins (x 6)**
Ice: **Cubes**
Garnish: **Red clover blossoms**

Serves 6 (approximately 1 quart/1 liter)

Bring the water to a slow boil in the nonreactive pan, add the clover blossoms, and gentle simmer for 5 minutes. Strain the liquid into the wide-mouthed pitcher, removing the blossoms, and return to the cleaned pan over a low heat. Add the lemon juice and honey, and stir to dissolve the honey. Do not let it boil. Remove from the heat and pour the lemonade into the cleaned pitcher. Chill for a couple of hours in the refrigerator. To serve, fill the 6 glasses with ice. Pour the lemonade three-quarters of the way up each one. Garnish with fresh red clover blossoms. Top with soda water and serve immediately.

Lavender HONEYSUCKLE

You can make this summer mocktail punch in quantity in advance and then top up everyone's glass with soda water on the day. As well as tasting delicious, it is also very good for you. Raw honey is rich in cancer-fighting phytonutrients and powerful antioxidants, found in the propolis that the bees use to sterilize the beehive. The acacia blossoms provide extra floral notes but aren't strictly necessary.

Tools: **Large nonreactive pan, wooden spoon, fine-strainer/ cheesecloth, large pitcher, ladle (optional)**

Glass: **Collins (x 6)**

Ice: **Cubes**

Garnish: **Lavender sprigs, lemon balm sprigs**

Serves 6 (makes approximately 1½ pints (750ml)

2 cups (640g) raw, runny honey

2 cups (500ml) warm water

2 heaped tbsp fresh edible-grade lavender buds or 4 tsp dried lavender blossoms

2 heads of acacia blossom (optional, if in season)

1 cup (250ml) freshly squeezed lemon juice

2 lemons, sliced into thin wheels

1 cup (20g) lemon balm (*Melissa officinalis*) or mint (*Mentha*) leaves

Splash of soda water

Combine the honey and water in the nonreactive pan and stir over a low heat until the honey liquefies and dissolves. Just before the liquid boils, add the lavender buds and acacia blossom heads (if you have them), remove the pan from the heat, and let steep for 20 minutes.

Strain the mixture using a fine-strainer or cheesecloth into the large pitcher (see page 26) to remove the lavender buds (and blossoms). Return the liquid to the cleaned pan, then add the lemon juice and the lemon wheels. Smack the lemon balm or mint leaves between your palms to release the essential oils. Add to the pan. Let stand for an hour.

If you wish, strain the mocktail punch again. Alternatively, remove the lemon balm or mint leaves and serve using a ladle, as we do at Midnight Apothecary. Fill 6 glasses with ice. Pour the punch two-thirds of the way up each glass. Top with a splash of soda water. Garnish with the sprigs of lavender and fresh sprigs of mint or lemon balm.

> It is claimed that local raw honey can help hay fever sufferers develop an immunity to the local pollen.
>
>
>
> If you don't pick the lavender yourself, make sure that you buy "edible grade" lavender, which has been handled hygienically.

Birch, Ginger & Wisteria
DETOXER

This mocktail is a great detoxer. Sap from the white birch (*Betula alba*) or silver birch (*Betula pendula*) is one of the healthiest juices you can drink. Unless you know how to harvest it yourself, online is your best place to source it. First impressions aren't good, though. It's a thin, slightly sweet, slightly bitter, herbal watery liquid, but its restorative and detoxifying properties are legendary. Unusually, it tackles the body's two cleansing and purification systems—the liver and kidneys—at the same time, and helps flush out harmful toxins, uric acid, and excess water from the body.

Its partner here is flavorsome ginger, with its own health-giving properties. Ginger fires up the digestive juices and, according to Ayurvedic texts, the libido! It also clears the sinuses, overcomes nausea and flatulence, and contains anti-inflammatory properties. Meanwhile, the wisteria flower garnish has a role here primarily for its looks—it's really pretty and the perfect blowzy opposite to the restrained, cloudy-looking tonic. It's also edible.

3oz (90ml) birch sap
1 oz (30ml) Ginger Syrup (see page 70)
¾oz (22ml) freshly squeezed lemon juice
Splash of soda water

Tools: **Cocktail shaker with strainer**
Glass: **Collins**
Ice: **Cubes**
Garnish: **Wisteria blossom**

Serves 1

Chill the glass thoroughly in the freezer or refrigerator for 2 or 4 hours respectively. Alternatively, fill the glass with ice.

Pour all the ingredients into the cocktail shaker and fill it two-thirds of the way up with ice. Cover and shake hard for 20 seconds. If you used ice to chill your glass, empty it out. Strain the cocktail into the glass. Garnish with the wisteria blossom and top with a splash of soda water.

> **Birch sap is high in potassium, calcium, phosphorus, magnesium, manganese, zinc, sodium, iron, and copper, not to mention vitamins B and C. On the down side, it has a very short shelf life (2–5 days), even if refrigerated, but it does freeze well.**

Good CALMER

Apple mint (*Mentha suaveolens*) was used by monks in the Middle Ages to treat epilepsy—they believed it calmed the brain. This mint has a delicate sweet aroma of spearmint and apple, and is actually considered superior in taste to spearmint (*M. spicata*) but lets itself down with its hairy leaves. We don't worry about that here—we embrace its fuzziness.

When it comes to the sweet herbal component of this drink, you can use either Elderflower Liqueur, in which case this drink will be mildly alcoholic, or Meadowsweet Syrup, if it's in season, for a nonalcoholic mocktail. Store-bought elderflower cordial will work just as well.

1 large handful apple mint leaves, stalks removed

2 large lemons, sliced into thin wheels

5oz (150ml) freshly squeezed lemon juice

7oz (200ml) Elderflower Liqueur (alcoholic, see page 57) or Meadowsweet Syrup (nonalcoholic, see page 86)

3 cups (750ml) organic cloudy apple juice

3 cups (750ml) soda water

Tools: **Large, wide-mouthed pitcher, muddler**

Glass: **Collins (x 6)**

Ice: **Cubes**

Garnish: **Apple mint sprigs, lemon wheels, elderflower/ meadowsweet blossoms**

Serves 6 (approximately 1 quart/1 liter)

Smack the mint leaves between your hands to release the essential oils, gently tear them, and drop into the pitcher. Add the lemon wheels, muddling them lightly (see page 33) to release some of their juice. Add the lemon juice, the Elderflower Liqueur or Meadowsweet Syrup, and apple juice. Give it a good stir and place the pitcher in the refrigerator for at least an hour to chill properly and allow the flavors to marry.

When you are ready to serve, fill 6 glasses with ice. Fill each one two-thirds of the way up with the mix and top with soda water. Garnish with lemon wheels, elderflower blossoms or meadowsweet blossoms (whichever are in season), and fresh apple mint sprigs.

There are records of meadowsweet being used medicinally since the 14th century—Chaucer mentions it in *The Knight's Tale*. It is used for maintaining healthy sinuses and treating sinusitis, influenza, diabetes, and rheumatism. It's a cooling, aromatic, and astringent herb, famous for relieving pain—it contains salicylic acid, the active ingredient in aspirin. Its glorious floral scent makes it a favorite perfume ingredient. If that's not impressive enough, it's also shown to have powerful antimicrobial benefits and be good at treating an acidic stomach and diarrhea.

Rosehip TODDY

I was given a variation of this toddy by a sympathetic friend when I had a cold and was feeling miserable. After a couple of swigs, life seemed much more bearable. It's been the go-to winter warmer ever since. Rosehip syrup is bursting with vitamin C, which is great to have on board to fight off winter bugs. I always put Scotch in my toddy but go with whatever spirit or booze works for you. Bourbon is another good match with rosehips.

Tools: **Teaspoon**

Glass: **Mug/heatproof glass with handle**

Garnish: **Candied rosehip (see page 35) or lemon slice (optional)**

Serves 1

2oz (60ml) Scotch or other spirit of your choice

1oz (30ml) Rosehip Syrup (see page 89)

½oz (15ml) freshly squeezed lemon juice

Boiling water

Pour the booze, Rosehip Syrup, and lemon juice in a mug or heatproof glass. Top with boiling water and stir. Garnish with a candied rosehip or lemon slice, if you can be bothered.

Tansy EVER AFTER

In ancient societies, tansy (*Tanacetum vulgare*) was considered a symbol of everlasting life. Here, it is used for its appetite-stimulating properties. Its aromatic and slightly bitter notes marry beautifully with the floral Rose Petal Syrup. The mint provides additional appetite stimulation, with refreshing sweet sharp notes to cut through the sweetness. Apple juice is just plain good for you and delicious (see Good Calmer, page 192).

2oz (60ml) organic cloudy apple juice

¾oz (22ml) freshly squeezed lemon juice

½oz (15ml) Tansy Syrup (see page 95)

½oz (15ml) Rose Petal Syrup (see page 75)

Dash of rose water

3oz (90ml) apple spritzer or soda water

Tools: **Cocktail shaker with strainer**
Glass: **Collins**
Ice: **Cubes**
Garnish: **Tansy flowers, rosebud, apple slice, mint sprig**

Serves 1

Fill the glass with ice. Pour all the ingredients (except the apple spritzer or soda water) into the cocktail shaker. Fill it two-thirds of the way up with ice, cover, and shake hard for 20 seconds. Strain the contents of the shaker into the Collins glass over the ice. Top with apple spritzer or soda water, and garnish with tansy flowers, rosebud, apple slice, and sprig of mint.

> Tansy was used in the past, but no longer, to alleviate pain for migraine headaches, rheumatism, and even trapped gas. The presence of trace amounts of thujone, which is a uterine stimulant, means it should not be consumed in quantity, during pregnancy, or if breast-feeding.
>
>
>
> Roses have traditionally been used as an antidepressant and mild sedative in teas and oils, as well as a component of perfume. Rose water is available from Middle Eastern and health food stores.

HAIL *the Kale*

Here we go with a rather delicious kale mojito. It may look the most pious cocktail you would never wish to drink but, aside from its extraordinary luminescent green color, I think you will be pleasantly surprised. A mojito traditionally uses mint, and this is no exception. Once again, ginger provides a strong flavor alongside the kale and rum, as well as being very good for you (see the Birch, Ginger, and Wisteria Detoxer, page 191). If you don't want the booze, just double up on the kale.

Kale has been called "the new beef," "a nutritional powerhouse," and "the queen of greens." It's certainly very high in fiber, rich in antioxidants, and packed with iron, magnesium, and other nutrients, as well as vitamins A and C, and omega-3 fatty acids. And, for anyone thinking they have to consume dairy to get their calcium intake, take a look at kale.

1 lime, cut into 6 wedges (2 for the garnish)

6 mint leaves (preferably spearmint)

¾oz (22ml) Ginger Syrup (see page 70)

2oz (60ml) white rum

2oz (60ml) kale juice (see right)

Splash of soda water

Tools: **Muddler**

Glass: **Collins**

Ice: **Cubes/crushed (see page 32)**

Garnish: **2 lime wedges, mint sprig, blackcurrant sage flower, anise hyssop blossom, and baby kale leaf (all optional)**

Serves 1

Place 4 lime wedges in the glass and muddle hard (see page 33) to release the juice (you need about 1½ tablespoons/25g of lime juice). Smack the mint leaves between your hands to release the essential oils, and add to the limes. Pour in the Ginger Syrup. Half-fill the glass with ice. Add the rum and kale juice, and garnish with the remaining 2 lime wedges and mint sprig. You can add flower garnishes and a baby kale leaf, if you wish (see left). Top with soda water and serve.

KALE JUICE

Take 2 large handfuls of fresh, washed, chopped kale and combine with about 1oz (30ml) water in a blender. Pulse on a high speed for 30 seconds until you have a bright green, smooth juice.

The queen of greens is thought to help in the fight against various cancers, Alzheimer's, inflammatory disorders, and more. It's also good for the skin, vision, immune system, metabolism, and hydration.

Fennel, Ginger,
AND LEMON THYME REVIVER

There is no sympathy to be doled out here for irresponsible drinking—just a practical hangover cure that is actually quite delicious. Fennel can help improve the function of your poor, overworked, toxin-laden liver. It's also been called the pearl of aphrodisiacs, so it might really perk you up! Ginger should help wake up your senses and overcome nausea. Thyme helps soothe muscles and stomach at the same time.

1 tsp fennel seeds

1 thumbnail-sized piece of ginger, thinly sliced or grated

3 x 3-in (8-cm) long lemon thyme sprigs

Boiling water

1 tsp honey, preferably raw, set or runny

Glass: **Teacup/heatproof glass with handle**

Garnish: **Thyme sprig, spear of freshly peeled ginger, fennel floret**

Serves 1

Place the fennel seeds, ginger, and sprigs of lemon thyme in the cup or heatproof glass. Pour over boiling water, almost to the top. Add the honey and stir. Garnish with a thyme sprig, ginger spear, and fennel floret.

The Flu BUSTER

Spoonfuls of elderberry syrup have been poured down children's (and adults')
throats over the centuries to fend off winter colds and flu. Elderberries are
said to boost the immune system, have antioxidant properties, and even
improve heart health. They are high in vitamin C, potassium, beta carotene,
calcium, and phosphorus. Cloves make an ideal pairing, reducing inflammation
and aiding digestion. Raw honey is just plain good for you (see Lavender
Honeysuckle, page 188), while ginger has antiviral properties. I serve this
hot with slices of fresh ginger to open up the sinuses.

> The reason why elderberries
> are said to tackle viral
> infections is that bioflavonoids
> and other proteins in the juice
> destroy the ability of cold and
> flu viruses to infect a cell.

**2oz (60ml) Elderberry and Clove
Syrup (see page 88)**
**1oz (30ml) Ginger Syrup
(see page 70)**
1 tsp (10ml) raw, set honey
6oz (180ml) boiling water

Tools: **Barspoon/long spoon**
Glass: **Mug/heatproof glass
with handle**
Garnish: **Spear of freshly
peeled ginger**

Serves 1

Measure the syrups and honey into
a mug or a heatproof glass. Pour
boiling water almost to the top and
stir hard until all the ingredients are
combined. Garnish with a spear of
fresh ginger. Add a slug of bourbon
or Scotch if you want to be sure of
fending off anything nasty!

ONLY *the* Mahonia

This dark, vaguely honey-scented syrup makes a wonderful mocktail. It could be called a Julep—it certainly looks like one and it's made in a julep cup and with a julep strainer—but, strictly speaking, that would be wrong, in part because we've chosen to make it nonalcoholic, using grape juice. The julep cup, though, is the perfect show-off vessel for draping over bunches of mahonia berries, bringing to mind an Ancient Greek bacchanalian feast.

1½oz (45ml) Mahonia Syrup (see page 85)

¾oz (22ml) freshly squeezed lime juice

5 mint leaves

2oz (60ml) red or white grape juice

Tools: **Cocktail shaker with strainer, julep strainer**

Glass: **Chilled julep cup**

Ice: **Cubes, crushed (see page 32)**

Garnish: **Raceme of mahonia berries, preferably Oregon grape (*Mahonia aquifolium*)**

Serves 1

Pour the Mahonia Syrup and lime juice into the cocktail shaker, fill it two-thirds of the way up with ice cubes, and shake hard for 20 seconds. Smack a mint leaf between your palms to release the essential oil and rub it around the edge of the chilled julep cup. Place it in the cup. Smack the remaining 4 mint leaves and place in the cup. Fill with crushed ice. Strain the mahonia and lime mix through the crushed ice in the glass to combine and further chill the drink. Top with red or white grape juice until just below the top of the crushed ice. Place the julep strainer inside the cup and garnish with the raceme of mahonia berries.

This cocktail is yet another appetite stimulator and booster of the immune system, but is to be avoided if you are pregnant or breast-feeding because of its uterine-stimulating properties.

Mahonia berries are high in vitamin C and, in the past, they were often used to treat scurvy. The alkaloids in it have been found to be antibacterial, antifungal, anti-inflammatory, antioxidant, and antidiarrheal.

Mahonia pairs beautifully with milder fruit like apples, pears, and grapes.

RESOURCES

BOOKS

The Forager's Handbook by Miles Irving, Ebury Press, 2009
A guide to the edible plants of Great Britain.

Food For Free by Richard Mabey, Collins, 1972
This is still the classic go-to reference book and has been revised with color photographs and turned into a Collins Gem pocket guide so that you can take it foraging.

Edible Wild Plants: A North American Field Guide by Thomas S. Elias and Peter A. Dykeman, Sterling, 1990
A very useful book for a wild food library because it provides 1–4 color photographs of each of the 220 wild plants it identifies, together with a range map and guide to each plant's uses.

A Field Guide to Edible Wild Plants: Eastern and Central North America by Lee Allen Peterson, Peterson Field Guide Series No 23, 1999
Usefully, this guide includes shrubs, trees, vines, and non-showy flowering plants that you might not find in a regular wildflower guide.

Jekka's Complete Herb Book by Jekka McVicar, Kyle Cathie, 2009
This is my go-to book for anyone who loves gardening and cooking. It has everything from planting plans, beautiful photography, tips on how to propagate, grow, prune, and harvest a huge selection of herbs, with a wealth of information on their culinary and medicinal applications.

WEBSITES

www.eatweeds.co.uk Robin Harford's Wild Food Guide to the edible plants of Britain. Fantastic resource with plenty of information on courses and recipes too.

www.gallowaywildfoods.com Mark Williams' site is absolutely jam-packed with wonderful tips, recipes, and knowledge about wild food and drink, and he is very generous in sharing knowledge from other websites and blogs around the world. Also provides great foraging trips in Scotland.

www.capitalgrowth.org Supporter of Midnight Apothecary when we needed some good topsoil and bursting with practical advice and support for food-growing communities in London.

www.theorchardproject.co.uk Another wonderful provider of information and support to encourage people to plant, care for, and harvest fruit trees across the U.K.

www.notfarfromthetree.org A Toronto-based project based around picking fruit and distributing it by bike throughout Toronto.

www.cityfruit.org A Seattle, community-based fruit project mapping existing trees and teaching people how to care for and maximize their harvests.

TWITTER ACCOUNTS

@KnowWildFood Canadian Dylan Gordon posts interesting tweets on the Canadian wild food industry and foraging in general.

@ReneRedzepiNoma Gourmet forager and founder of Noma, who is still tweeting inspiring dishes and wild ingredients from around the world.

@SummerStarCoop A U.S. forager/farmer perspective.

@markwildfood Mark Williams of www.gallowaywildfoods.com tweets updates of his incredible wild food and drink forays—very entertaining.

@foragefinefoods Liz Knight manages to be informative and entertaining while balancing childcare (literally) as she works.

EDIBLE FLOWERS

www.maddocksfarmorganics.co.uk Huge variety of organic edible flowers grown by Jan Billington in Devon, England.

COCKTAIL COURSES

www.themidnightapothecary.co.uk Cheeky plug for my website! I run courses and master classes from time to time, so check out the website or contact me if you would like something bespoke.

FORAGED FOOD AND INGREDIENTS

www.foragefinefoods.com Exquisite small-batch syrups, spice blends and rubs made by Liz Knight in Herefordshire, England.

www.forager.org.uk U.K. supplier of wild plants, funghi, and syrups.

FORAGING COURSES AND EXPERTS IN THE U.K.

twitter.com/jonthepoacher What Jonathan Cook doesn't know about wild edibles on Walthamstow Marshes isn't worth knowing! Very helpful guide and mentor.

www.foragelondon.co.uk John Rensten, forager and blogger who leads foraging walks in and around London.

www.coastalsurvival.com In addition to running bushcraft courses, Fraser Christian is a fully qualified chef and professional forager, who runs wonderful foraging courses in the U.K.

www.fathen.org A wild cookery school in west Cornwall run by botanist and chef Caroline Davey. Caroline will take you for beautiful foraging forays and teach you how to identify and cook your treasures to perfection.

HERBS AND ESSENTIAL OILS (CATERING GRADE)

www.wildharvestuk.com U.K. suppliers to the catering trade of unusual herbs, edible flowers, and edible flower extracts such as jasmine.

www.mountainroseherbs.com U.S. supplier of organic herbs (including ethically wild-harvested and Kosher certified botanical products), spices, looseleaf teas, essential oils, and herbal extracts.

www.dandelionbotanical.com U.S. natural apothecary supplying certified organic herbs, spices, and botanicals.

LIQUEURS

www.bramleyandgage.com Makers of fruit gins and fruit liqueurs with no added colorings or preservatives in Devon, England.

www.somersetciderbrandy.com Makers of cider, cider brandy, apple eau de vie, and morello cherries in eau de vie, based in Somerset, England.

GIN

www.bermondseygin.com Jensen's Gin distillers are based just around the corner from Midnight Apothecary. Distillers of superb Old Tom gin, made to an unsweetened 1840's recipe, and a lovely London Bermondsey Dry.

BEER

www.hiverbeers.com Hiver, the Honey Beer, is a beautifully delicate and floral beer using rural and urban honey. Based in southeast London and regular supporters of Midnight Apothecary!

SMALL BATCH AND RARE LIQUOR

www.gerrys.uk.com Gerry's Wines and Spirits are based in the heart of Soho, London. If you can't find what you're looking for anywhere else, they are bound to have it!

ICE CREAM

www.rubyviolet.co.uk London-based creators of handmade ice cream and sorbet in the most exquisite flavors. Can provide frozen ice cream spheres—perfect for dropping into a dessert cocktail.

MIXOLOGY AND GOURMET CATERING EQUIPMENT

www.cocktailkingdom.com Online suppliers of every conceivable piece of bar equipment you might need, from shakers to julep cups to dashers, bitters, and books.

www.modernistpantry.com Website supplying flavor pearls and a wide range of mixology kits/chemicals to make your own, as well as supplying professional cream whippers.

www.nisbets.co.uk Huge selection of catering and bar equipment.

www.ebay.com A huge range of vintage and collectible bar tools, equipment, and glasses.

ORGANIC INGREDIENTS

www.abelandcole.co.uk Incredible range of U.K. home-delivered organic fruit, herbs, and dairy—and even organic booze. Also have a wonderful YouTube channel at www.youtube.com/abelandcole.

MIDNIGHT APOTHECARY POP-UP BAR

www.facebook.com/MidnightApothecary
twitter.com/LottieMuir The Midnight Apothecary pop-up cocktail bar is based at the Brunel Museum in southeast London. Visit the Facebook page or my Twitter account to find out when events are taking place.

MIXOLOGY ONLINE CHANNELS

www.youtube.com/JamiesDrinksTube
www.youtube.com/ABarAbove

GLOSSARY

Additional terms are covered in more detail in Chapter One (see pages 26–39).

ABV
(Alcohol by Volume) A standard measure of how much alcohol (ethanol) is contained in a drink, expressed as a percentage of total volume.

ANNUAL
A plant that lives for less than a year.

APÉRITIF
A drink taken before a meal with a bitter element, to stimulate the appetite.

CITRIC ACID
The primary acid from citrus fruit.

COBBLER
Usually a spirit or wine, plus sugar, served over crushed ice, often garnished with fruit.

COCKTAIL
Two hundred years ago, a cocktail was liquor, bitters, sugar, and water—nothing else. Now it's a catchall phrase for any mixed drink containing alcohol.

COLLINS
A Sour topped with soda, served in a long glass filled with ice.

DASH
A one-flick motion with the bottle, as you would add soy sauce. If using bitters with a dropper, use two drops for one dash.

EXTRACT
An extract is a herbal infusion made by macerating a herb with high-proof alcohol or vegetable glycerin in a ratio of 1 part herb to 1 part alcohol or glycerin.

FIZZ
Same as a Collins, except a Fizz is usually shaken, strained, and served without ice. Can also refer to a drink where soda water has been added. Also slang for sparkling wine.

FLAVOR PEARLS
(or "caviar spheres") Drops of fruity, salty, or spicy juices trapped in a thin alginate shell designed to release their flavor as they burst in your mouth. Available from online mixology and gourmet catering suppliers in a range of sweet and savory flavors.

INFUSION
The process of extracting flavor, aromatics, vitamins, and minerals from soft ingredients (flowers, leaves, roots, or citrus peel) into a solvent (alcohol, water, sugar, wine, vinegar, or oil). I use the term interchangeably to refer to cold infusions, such as infusing flowers in gin to make a flavored gin, like False Acacia Gin (see page 50) or to hot infusions, where herbs are simmered in sugar and water to make a syrup, like Chocolate Mint Syrup (see page 80).

JULEP
Originally a medicinal drink, containing liquor (often bourbon), mint, and crushed ice.

MACERATION
A cold infusion where a soft herb/fruit is steeped in a solvent such as alcohol, or where fruit is put in sugar at room temperature in a container excluded from light.

Maceration is also used to refer to the process of infusing fruit with alcohol, for example, brandied plums or cherries. I specifically refer to maceration in the section about using fruit and sugar together to produce a liquid (see pages 42–43)—I think of it as something done in the dark at room temperature with soft fruit.

MALIC ACID
The primary acid from unripe tree fruit like crab apples.

PEEL
Citrus zest combined with the white pith below.

PERENNIAL
A plant that lives for an indefinite length of time, but longer than one year. May flower and fruit many times.

pH
The measure of alkalinity or acidity on a scale of 1–14, where 7 is neutral.

PROOF
The measure of alcohol in wine or spirits. 100% = approximately 50 ABV.

SOUR
A spirit, plus citrus and sugar (usually in a 2:1:1 ratio), and sometimes egg white.

SMASH
Same as a Julep, but with the addition of citrus and fruit.

STERILIZE
A process of cleaning to remove bacteria, wild yeasts, and other contaminants.

TINCTURE
The same process as an extract but with a ratio of 1 part herb to 3 parts alcohol or glycerin, which is then filtered and diluted to end up with a finished product of about 25% alcohol.

ZEST
The colorful part of citrus fruit, where all the aromatic oils are stored.

INDEX

ACKNOWLEDGMENTS

My gratitude to: Sally Powell, the art director at CICO Books, who sipped a cocktail and suggested a book; to Cindy Richards, who made it happen; to Carmel Edmonds for being a patient editor; and to Helen Ridge for being a very supportive, chivvying, and enthusiastic copy-editor. Big thanks to photographer Kim Lightbody, who thinks nothing of hiking equipment through a dewy field at dawn on Walthamstow Marshes before making some very classy compositions.

A huge thank you to the Midnight Apothecary crew who have made Saturday nights at the bar so magical: Heather, Ashley, Dan, Ella, Liam, Suse, Jack, HuiHui, Harunobu, Janet, Katie, and Tim. Thanks to the wonderful Dr. Anne at Jensen's Gin in Bermondsey for supporting the bar and trying to teach me how to make flavor pearls; to Hannah of Hiver Honey Beer fame for the delicious beer and support. To Caroline, Catherine, and Julith for rescuing the first Midnight Apothecary from certain disaster when 120 people turned up instead of the dozen we'd expected. To Robert Hulse, the director of the Brunel Museum, for allowing and supporting me to build the garden and then encouraging me ever since. To Jonathan Cook, for wonderful foraging trips and bounty on Walthamstow Marshes. To my lovely brother David and niece Ruby, for finding and whittling marshmallow sticks. To my Canadian "family" at the lake who tested the drinks and provided such a beautiful place to write over the summer: Linda, Mark, Diane, John, Allie, and all the pups.

To the Midnight Apothecary guests who keep on coming and making it so much fun. To my mum for her creativity, boundless energy, and zest for life, which will stay with me forever. And, finally, and most of all, to my favorite blackberry Martini maker, adventurer, washer-upper, nudger, supporter, and rock: EJ.

PICTURE CREDITS